The LANCASHIRE Cook Book

A celebration of the amazing food and drink on our doorstep.
Featuring over 45 stunning recipes.

The Lancashire Cook Book

©2016 Meze Publishing. All rights reserved.

First edition printed in 2016 in the UK.

ISBN: 978-1-910863-09-1

Thank you to: Andrew Nutter, Nutters Restaurant, Dawn Holding Hospitality Action, John Gillmore BBC Radio Lancashire, Nigel Barden BBC Radio 2, Simon Wood.

Compiled by: Anna Tebble

Written by: Karen Dent

Photography by:
Tim Green (www.timgreenphotographer.co.uk)

Edited by: Rachel Heward, Phil Turner

Designed by: Marc Barker, Paul Cocker

Cover art: Luke Prest, www.lukeprest.com

Contributors: Faye Bailey, Kerre Chen, Sarah Koriba, Holly Vincent

Printed by Bell and Bain Ltd, Glasgow

Published by Meze Publishing Limited
Unit 1 Beehive Works
Milton Street
Sheffield S3 7WL
Web: www.mezepublishing.co.uk
Tel: 0114 275 7709
Email: info@mezepublishing.co.uk

CONTENTS

Editorial

Credits	4
Foreword by Andrew Nutter, Nutters Restaurant	8
Welcome to Lancashire	12
Hospitality Action	34
The directory	214

Guest recipes

John Gillmore
Proper Lancashire hotpot	146

Nigel Barden
A taste of home	156
Jacobs ladder	158

Saddleworth WI
So much more than jam and Jerusalem	182
Banana and pecan loaf	184

Simon Wood
A master chef	192
Pork belly with marvellous mash, broad beans and asparagus	194

Chef recipes

Visit Lancashire
A taste of the county	16
Top taste destinations	18
Foodie festivals	20
Cheese please	24
Raise a glass to real ale	26
Awards all round	28
Goosnargh chicken with black garlic, mushrooms and asparagus	30
Risotto with green tea and Morecambe bay shrimps	32

Albion Farm Shop
Home produced and hand picked	38
Cheese and onion pie	42
Rag pudding	44

Barton Grange Garden Centre
Locally grown	46
Lancaster lemon tart	48

Bashall Barn Farm Shop
Homemade heaven	50
Braised blade of beef	52

Be Chocolate
Crème fraîche mousse with spiced mango purée	56

Bertram's Restaurant
Destination dining	58
Lemon and buttermilk scones	60
Sesame salmon yakisoba	62
Pistachio and white chocolate brownie	64

The Bird at Birtle
Perfect pub grub	66
Brill, wild garlic pesto, Formby asparagus, fermented black garlic and lemon dressing	68

The Blue Mallard
Canalside classics	70
Smoked cod with Southport shrimp souffle served with buttered kale, Mrs Kirkham's Lancashire cheese and leek croquettes with watercress sauce	72
Melting chocolate fondant with white chocolate and honeycomb parfait	74

Brown's the Butchers
Quality mix of traditional and modern	76
Braised haggis stuffed pork belly	78

The Bury Black Pudding Company

    The only Bury Black Pudding on the block   80

    Lamb hotpot with black pudding   82

Butler's Farmhouse Cheeses

    The daddy of blue cheeses   84

    Blacksticks Blue beef stroganoff   88

The Cartford Inn

    A French influence in Lancashire   90

    Pilling Marsh lamb breast with black peas, sweetbreads, sheep's curd cheese, pea purée and a wild garlic and mint dressing   92

Cowman's Famous Sausage

    Sausage heaven   94

    Cajun melting mozzarella meatballs   96

Dearden Tea Rooms

    A warm welcome   98

    Sticky toffee pudding   100

duk-pond

    Quirky, creative and contemporary   102

    Peruvian stew   104

    Machu Picchu   106

Exchange Coffee

    A cup of something special   108

    Clever Dripper brew guide   110

Gazegill Organics

    As nature intended   112

    Rose veal escalope   118

Gibbon Bridge Hotel

    Simple elegance   120

    Loin of lamb topped with a spinach and mint mousse with a puff pastry lattice   122

Henry's Bar and Grill, Capri and Barrique

    A trio of tastes   124

    Lamb hash with lamb chops   126

    Ham croquetas   128

    Chorizo and 'nduja risotto   130

Huntley's Country Stores

    From farm shop to restaurant   132

    Beef short ribs   134

    Wild mushrooms on toast with a creamy mustard sauce   138

The Inn at Whitewell

    Chill out in the countryside   140

    Pan-fried king scallops   142

    Confit shoulder of lamb and Jersey Royal terrine   144

Made in Lancashire

    Power in numbers   148

    Goatherd's pie   150

Mrs Dowson's Ice Cream

    The ice cream lady   152

    Mrs Dowson's perfect pancakes and ice cream   154

Nutters Restaurant

    Not just a meal, but an adventure   160

    Honey roast Goosnargh duck breast, leg meat pithivier and cauliflower frits   162

Preston BID

    Love food, love Preston   164

    Nineteen 75 Bury black pudding, poached egg, hollandaise   166

Procter's Choice

    The cheese factor   168

    Kick-ass tartlets   170

Puddleducks Tea room

    A hidden gem at the centre of the kingdom   172

    Famous pea and ham soup   174

The Red Pump Inn

    Superb steak and quality classics   176

    Prime rib steak and chimichurri sauce   178

Samlesbury Hall

    A feast for the eyes and the tastebuds   186

    Twice-cooked confit of duck with rabenda jus   188

    Roasted Mediterranean vegetables   190

The Village Tea Room at Wheelton

    The perfect excuse to indulge   196

    Classic fruit scone   198

The White Horse

    Stand and deliver   200

    Stuffed free-range chicken   202

The Yew Tree Inn

    Destination: Lancashire   204

    Ricotta with balsamic glaze, dried herbs and sourdough bread   206

    Pan-roast lamb canon   208

    Blood orange cheesecake   210

FOREWORD

What's for tea mum?

And when the reply came back 'Lancashire hotpot', eyes widened and bellies rumbled in anticipation of the family feast ahead. The Nutter clan sat around the wooden kitchen table in silence as the joy of the first mouthful of slow cooked lamb was devoured along with chunks of bread to mop up the rich stock gravy, and of course the obligatory pickled red cabbage. Such memories!

Lancashire fare is tasty, comforting and full of surprises; whether it's those traditional stews and casseroles or slightly more obscure cuts of meat like tripe, cow heel and lamb fry. There's more to the Red Rose County than meets the eye.

The great thing about Lancashire food is the producers who grow and rear the produce. For example the county is known for its great cheese names like Kirkham's, Sandham's and Butler's. When I work abroad, it's great to see Lancashire cheese on the menu and it takes you back to being a kid, and toasting crumpets with cheese melting on the top. Of course, things like Bury black pudding and Goosnargh duck feature heavily in my childhood memories too.

Nowadays, eating out in Lancashire is hugely popular, and has rocketed in the last few years especially. This is based on more discerning diners, and their appetite for good quality ingredients. It's up the pubs, restaurants and cafés of the region to take these raw materials and showcase them in the best possible way.

When we took over Nutters Restaurant, it had been a chain eatery. But it was clear people were beginning to demand a bit more than a carbon copy menu, so we changed our approach in order to create a truly unique and enjoyable experience for customers – using the finest produce on our doorstep.

It's important to keep up the standards of what we're true to in Lancashire. That means staying with local and regional food and passing on compliments to the farmers, because at the end of the day, a lot of people take it for granted. There's nothing better than someone saying 'that duck was amazing, where did you get it from?' and telling them so they can go to the farmer and cook it at home.

And whilst eating out in your local area is important, so too is home cooking. My mum was a home economics teacher and she got us so fired up about cooking. It annoys me now that some schools aren't prioritising cookery as a fundamental skill. When I was at school, you made the pastry and stewed the apples down for a pie. You went in with your wicker basket and there was a joy to be found in the aromas of the cookery class, wandering around to see what everyone else's was like and saying: 'yes, that's mine' when the teacher took the pies out of the oven. Naturally, I was the class swot in cookery.

Now kids make pies with pre-made pastry and tins of stewed apples. That's not cooking that's assembling, and there's no skill there. Unfortunately that's the way it's going, though some schools are beginning to challenge this, which is encouraging.

We should be teaching our children that food is one of the greatest things that can bring us together. So try your hand at one of the recipes in this book and when you're digging in with all of your family around the table, having a chat with your mobile phones switched off, you'll realise there's nothing better.

Andrew Nutter

Welcome to LANCASHIRE

From coast and countryside to city, there's a world of flavours
to discover in the North West.

The Red Rose County of Lancashire is a place of many parts.

Famed as the hub of industrial revolution, the dark satanic cotton mills and coal mines are long gone – and so too are the big cities of Manchester and Liverpool into metropolitan counties of their own. Today, this corner of North West England can lay claim to providing a mix of everything, with lively urban centres to lush countryside and coasts.

Blessed with fish and shellfish from the coast, a strong dairy, beef-rearing and vegetable growing tradition in the lowlands, and lamb and game from the hills, you can discover the ingredients for a great meal without ever going over the county boundary.

The county is justly famed for its Lancashire cheese – which comes in the three varieties of tasty, creamy and crumbly. Of course, you can't think Lancashire without thinking hotpot, but it's also home to traditional black pudding and some of the most sought after sausages in the UK.

The foodie traditions that are still alive today benefit from the abundance of flavours and ingredients – but are also drawn from a past where poverty and hunger were no stranger to many working families. Chefs and butchers will tell you that many of the county's traditional dishes are based on making the most of what was available, so hotpots, cheese and onion pies, rag puddings and black peas were key parts of the diet.

Gastropubs and country inns are making a real name for themselves with adventurous dishes using local and seasonal ingredients; coffee shops and tea rooms are creating superb afternoon tea experiences; and restaurants are preparing quirky and delightful takes on the classics.

Many farm shops sprang up after the 2001 foot and mouth crisis and today are thriving enterprises, with their own cafés and restaurants enthusiastically showcasing what you can create from the marvellous products they sell.

It's that spirit that has fuelled the chefs, cooks, bakers, farmers and food producers and their recipes that fill the Lancashire Cook Book. You'll discover old favourites nestled among new ideas; simple lunches and suppers, ambitious dinner party dishes, proper puddings and teatime baked treats.

We aim to take you on a journey through the many faces of Lancashire food today and capture your imagination to get cooking with some of the very best ingredients you'll find anywhere in Britain. Whatever your level of culinary expertise, you'll find recipes to excite, enthuse, challenge – and most of all, enjoy.

Dig in!

A Taste of the COUNTY

From coast to countryside via hills, moorland and forests, Lancashire's stunning scenery has resulted in a superb basket of ingredients and a foodie heritage second to none.

It's no secret that Lancashire is one of the best counties for sourcing quality food and drink, with fabulous products unique to the area that have been made here for generations.

Visit Lancashire likes to point out that life really does taste good across here, whether you're looking for ingredients that are grown, caught, reared or made locally. Abundance, quality, provenance and crucially, the passion of producers – something you'll hear about again and again in Lancashire – all combine to create a county that is a must-visit on the foodie map.

Lancashire has the distinction of not just being famed for one type of food. Although the Lancashire hotpot is of course ubiquitous, so too are its creamy, crumbly and tasty cheeses – made in the traditional way with local milk – shrimps from Morecambe Bay, Goosnargh chicken, superb meat from heather-reared Bowland lambs, rare breed pigs and superb beef steaks, sausages and of course black pudding.

You'll find 10 Lancashire cheese makers all within 10 miles of the Forest of Bowland Area of Outstanding Natural Beauty, including Grandma Singletons and Dewlay which makes the Protected Designator of Origin Beacon Fell traditional Lancashire cheese.

The county also lays claim to be the original home of the sirloin steak. Legend tells that King James I stayed at Hoghton Tower in 1617 and so enjoyed his meal, he knighted the beef. The banqueting hall where he ate the 'Sir Loin' can still be seen and visitors can stay the night in the Irishman's Tower.

The royal connection continues with Baxters of Morecambe Bay, who have been making traditional potted shrimps since 1880 and have held a Royal Warrant since 1967.

So much of the county's food heritage is due to its natural assets: fish and shellfish from the stunning coastline; lamb and game from the hills and salt marshes; top quality beef and dairy cattle grazing in the lush pastures; and the fertile lowlands where fruit and vegetables are produced and thanks to those aforementioned passionate farmers, producers, makers and chefs, the unique combination of superb scenery and top quality food makes a visit to Lancashire memorable on so many levels.

For more information visit www.VisitLancashire.com.

Top Taste DESTINATIONS

Take a tasty trip to Lancashire's cafés and tea rooms, destination venues, gastropubs, city bars and country inns, farmers' shops and markets.

Lancashire isn't just packed with superb flavours and authentic ingredients, but it also has the talent to make the very best of them. You'll find menus groaning with the great tastes of the county from super village cafés and tea rooms filled with homemade cakes, treats and posh afternoon teas, to inns with local craft ale and traditional and gastropub menus.

There is an abundance of real foodie inns, where you can enjoy local, seasonal and perfectly-produced food and drink. For a meal with a view, the Cartford Inn, Gibbon Bridge Hotel, Parkers Arms, the Red Pump Inn and the Inn at Whitewell will tick all the boxes. Plus, you can stay overnight and tuck into a fantastic Lancashire breakfast in the morning.

Destination venues abound such as Samlesbury Hall, Huntley's Country Stores, Barton Grange Garden Centre, Bashall Barn and the Café at Stydd Gardens, which provide a combination of a great meal and a great day out.

Lancashire's not short on sophistication either. Bertram's Restaurant, the Blue Mallard, duk-pond and Exchange Coffee provide a taste of quality, and the county boasts plenty of foodie award winners too. Northcote has a coveted Michelin Star and the Freemasons at Wiswell has twice taken the top spot in the Good Food Guide's Top 50 Pubs. The Seafood Pub Company's Oyster and Otter was named Best Food Pub by the Great British Pub Awards and its Assheton Arms was the 2014 Lancashire Tourism Pub of the Year.

Perfectly prepared food made from Lancashire ingredients is an affordable treat for locals and visitors alike. But you can also enjoy choosing your own fresh, seasonal produce to take home from one of the many superb farm shops or regular farmers' markets that take place across the county. Food events run throughout the year, where you can discover a new taste from artisan produced cheeses and baked goodies, to locally-reared meat and vegetables gathered straight from the fields. And don't forget Lancashire's strong butchery tradition, where succulent sausages and black pudding are among the specialities.

You can find out more at www.VisitLancashire.com.

Barton Grange Farm Shop

The Inn at Whitewell

Bertram,s

Exchange Coffee

Bowtons The Butchers

Gibbon Bridge

Foodie festivals and MARKETS

Whatever time of year you visit, you'll find food-focused events celebrating the ingredients and produce that is grown, reared or made in the county.

In a county so steeped in culinary traditions and top quality produce, it's only natural that Lancashire has a thriving food scene.

Set in the grounds of the magnificent Grade 1 listed building, Stonyhurst College near Clitheroe provides a stunning venue for a food and drink festival. The Great British Food Festival takes place in April over three days and attracts countless producers showcasing the best in local, seasonal and speciality food and drink. It's a great opportunity to get a real taste of the best of Lancashire produce.

The annual Accrington Food and Drink Festival held in June showcases the area's finest food producers and retailers and live cookery demonstrations with a celebrity chef for a day filled with flavours and family fun.

The Clitheroe Food Festival takes place in August each year, this one day event completely takes over the town and provides an absolute feast for the senses. Clitheroe's main street is closed off to traffic for the event and a special park and ride service is organised for the visitors who flock for a taste of the county's best flavours.

The festival brings together food and drink producers from the town and across the beautiful Ribble Valley with inspiring chefs demonstrating new ways to use ingredients, a massive street buffet and musical accompaniment while you explore.

Local farmers' markets are an important part of the small producer's route to market and a great way for food lovers to find a regular supply of wonderful and unique tastes. Noted for the quality of their fine locally produced stock, cheeses and meat products, some of the markets take place in the beautiful grounds of historic houses, like Hoghton Tower.

Established for more than 10 years, Hoghton Tower was one of the first historic houses in the country to recognise the importance of promoting high-quality local produce through a farmers' market. Running on the third Sunday of every month you can stock up on your favourite goodies and try something new.

For more information about these festivals and markets, and of course many more that happen right across the county, go to www.VisitLancashire.com, where dates and times of key markets are listed.

Cheese PLEASE

Lancashire can lay claim to being Britain's most famous cheese-making county and is home to both thriving major producers and artisan cheese makers.

Lancashire is synonymous with top quality British cheese. Unlike other cheeses that bear their county's name, Lancashire boasts three distinct types: tasty, creamy and crumbly.

The county's cheese-making heritage stems from Lancashire's proud dairy farming history. Many recipes that have been passed through the generations were originally created on the farmhouse kitchen table to feed the family or take to market to supplement the farm's income.

Today, those same recipes are being used, tweaked and perfected by cheese makers of all sizes. In recent years, Lancashire has enjoyed an explosion in new cheese production, with different recipes to tempt the taste buds now available alongside the traditional favourites. Whether you choose an artisan, farmhouse-produced cheese at a farmers' market or opt for a tried and tested big producer, you're guaranteed to be buying some of the best loved British cheeses.

Lancashire's best known cheese names include Greenfields, Mrs Kirkham's, Leagrams, Dewlay and Butler's.

Dewlay's Special Reserve Tasty Lancashire is a Gold Award winner in the International Cheese Awards, and the company is on the map as one of the UK's first wind-powered cheese makers thanks to its 126m high turbine. You can see it in action and watch cheese being made at the Dewlay Visitor Centre before stocking up in the shop.

Greenfields is a traditional family-run business that has been producing cheese since the 1930s, using family recipes that are big award winners. Its Traditional Crumbly Lancashire Cheese was crowned Supreme Champion at the International Cheese Awards 2015.

For organic cheeses, check out Leagram Organic Dairy. The business produces cheeses by hand, which are finished by dipping in hot wax to seal in the flavour. Its Organic Creamy Lancashire scooped a Gold Award at the International Cheese Awards, and the company is always developing new flavours with tasty additions including ginger, garlic, mint, apricot and mixed peppers.

You'll find Lancashire-produced cheeses on the cheeseboard and on the menu of some of the finest eateries across the county.

More information at www.VisitLancashire.com.

Raise a Glass
TO REAL ALE

Tasty brews made the traditional way are a real highlight of Lancashire's food and drink heritage.

If you have a taste for real ale, you're probably well aware of Lancashire's contribution to some of Britain's finest brews. But did you know the county was also the birthplace of the temperance movement?

Today, the UK's only remaining temperance bar – Fitzpatrick's – can be found in Rawtenstall, and the county's pubs and bars are packed with locally-made cask ales and brews from the 24 breweries and microbrewers based in Lancashire.

Whether you're a fan of chocolaty stouts, floral blonde beers, barley wines, bitters or golden ales, you're sure to find something different to whet your whistle. And one of the best ways to do it is by taking the East Lancashire Railway Real Ale Trail, which stops at a string of pubs between Bury and Rawtenstall, to sample their wares.

Perhaps Lancashire's most famous ale is Pendle Witches Brew, named after the Pendle witches who were tried and hanged in 1612. It's made with traditional techniques by Moorhouse brewery in Burnley, which was set up by William Moorhouse in 1865.

You can discover the secrets of making real ale at the Lancaster Brewery, which makes beer, cider and lager and offers guided tours for visitors. There's an opportunity for tasting sessions too, where you can enjoy a tipple with a selection of locally made pies. The brewery also has a visitors' centre, where you can see the hops used to make the beer growing outside, and buy your own supplies of ale to take home.

Also going from strength to strength is Bowland Brewery which started life as a micro-brewery and now supplies many pubs, bars and restaurants. Not just locally, but across the country the finest ingredients and an obsessive attention to detail still remain the guiding principles today.

Although brewing is an ancient art, there has been an upsurge in micro brewing in recent years and one of Lancashire's finest exponents is the Old School Brewery. Originally started as a hobby brewery by Ian Walsh and Ren Wallbank in 2012, it now produces handcrafted ales from its base at the foot of Warton Crag in north Lancashire that are sold at pubs across the county.

More information at www.VisitLancashire.com.

Awards
ALL ROUND

Lancashire's quality places to eat, drink and stay boast a string
of awards for excellence.

Lancashire is a superb spot if you're seeking fabulous food combined with a great place to stay – and our pubs and inns have the awards to prove it.

The Lancashire Tourism Awards has a category devoted to the county's Best Tourism Pubs and the Taste Lancashire County winners go forward to represent Lancashire at the annual Visit England Awards for Excellence to compete for the national honours. Winning a Tourism Pub Award means a venue has made a significant contribution to tourism and its local community, and that you'll find a great range of drinks and quality, locally-sourced food inside.

Lancashire Tourism Pubs of the Year have a strong record of success when they've gone on to represent the county in the national finals. In 2015, the Freemasons at Wiswell won gold, the highest award at the Visit England Excellence Awards. The country pub and shooting lodge in the Ribble Valley has seasonal and tasting menus alongside its a la carte favourites.

The Cartford Inn was a Tourism Pub of the Year and silver award winner in Visit England Awards in 2016. You'll find British cuisine with a French feel at the 17th century coaching inn, located on a scenic crossing of the River Wyre.

Taste Lancashire award winner La Locanda Ristorante Italiano at Gisburn also achieved bronze in the 2016 Visit England Awards. It provides a traditional taste of Italy in rural Lancashire, using mainly locally-sourced ingredients, with unspoilt views of The Forest of Bowland.

The Parkers Arms at Newton in Bowland was presented with a Taste Lancashire Award in 2013 and 2014 and followed that up with a highly commended in the 2015 Visit England Awards. It's a welcoming country inn focused on seasonal local ingredients.

Finally, check out The Assheton Arms in Clitheroe, winner of the county's 2013 Tourism Pub Award found in the conservation village of Downham, it boasts views of Pendle Hill and a traditional country pub ambience with daily changing specials on the menu.

To find out more go to www.VisitLancashire.com.

Visit Lancashire

The Cartford Inn

The Freemasons Arms

The Parkers Arms

The Assheton Arms

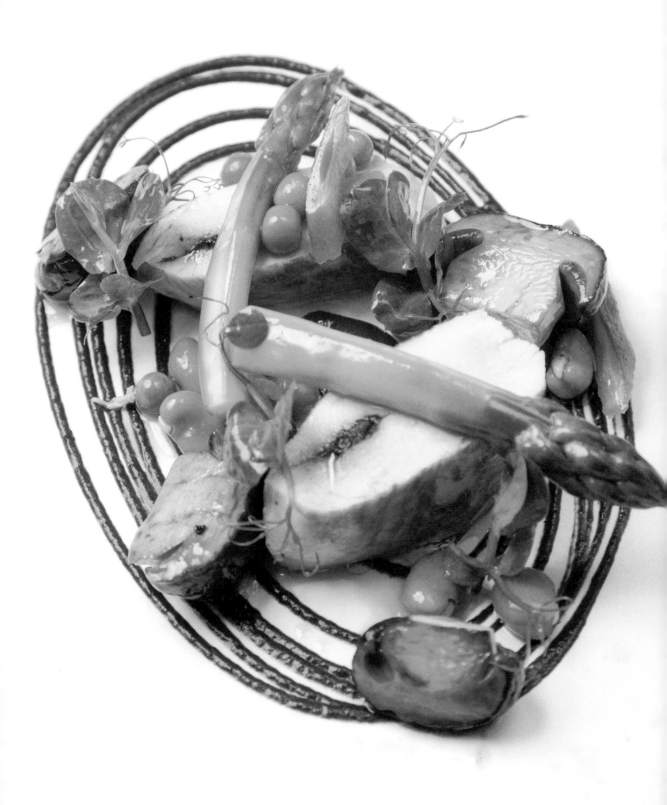

Visit Lancashire

GOOSNARGH CHICKEN WITH BLACK GARLIC, MUSHROOMS & ASPARAGUS

A tasty treat for two from Steven Smith, chef-proprietor of The Freemasons at Wiswell, twice rated No1 in the Good Food Guide Top 50 Pubs and 2015 Visit England Gold Award winner. Serves 2.

Ingredients

For the chicken:

2 Goosnargh chicken breasts, skin on

4 cloves black garlic

For the foie gras sauce:

250g foie gras, deveined and roughly chopped

400ml Gewürztraminer wine

585ml whole milk

1 lemon, juiced

Seasoning

For the charred leek purée:

4 white leeks

1 tbsp squid ink

1 tbsp miso paste

1 dash soy sauce

To serve:

4 chestnut mushrooms

1 knob butter

4 asparagus spears

100g broad beans

100g fresh peas

2-3 handfuls of pea shoots

Rapeseed oil

Salt

Method

For the foie gras sauce

Place 375ml of the wine in a saucepan and reduce to 100ml. In a separate pan, bring the milk to the boil slowly.

Remove from the heat and using a stick blender, blend in the foie gras, followed by the reduced wine and the juice of a lemon. Season to taste and set aside in a warm place until ready to serve.

For the charred leek purée

Cut the leeks in half lengthways and wash thoroughly. Use a very hot chargrill pan to blacken the leeks on both sides, then remove from the heat, trim down slightly and scatter evenly on the base of a saucepan.

Add enough water to just cover (200-300ml), bring to a boil and simmer until the liquid has reduced and the pan is almost dry. Transfer to a high-speed blender and blitz with the squid ink, a dash of soy sauce and the miso paste.

Once the purée is very smooth, press through a fine strainer, transfer to a squeezy bottle and set aside until required.

For the chicken

Preheat the oven to 150°C.

Make a couple of incisions along the side of each chicken breast and stuff with the black garlic. Bake in the oven for 18 minutes, then remove and rest for 5 minutes.

For the vegetables

Cut the chestnut mushrooms in half and colour cut-side down in a hot pan with a dash of rapeseed oil. To finish, add a small knob of butter, toss to coat and season with salt.

Trim the asparagus and peel up to the tip. Blanch in boiling salted water with the peas and broad beans for 1½ minutes. Strain, peel the broad beans, season all the greens and keep warm.

To serve

Before serving, reheat the foie gras sauce, adding the remaining 25ml of wine to refresh the flavour.

Pipe the charred leek purée in swirls on the base of each plate. Slice each breast in half and place on top of the purée.

Scatter the asparagus, broad beans, peas and mushrooms onto each plate. Drizzle with the foie gras sauce and garnish with pea shoots before serving.

Visit Lancashire
RISOTTO WITH GREEN TEA AND MORECAMBE BAY SHRIMPS

An Italian classic with a Lancashire flavour, which uses green tea instead of the usual stock. From 2016 Visit England Bronze Taste Award winner La Locanda, one of just 75 UK Italian restaurants to be awarded the Ospitalita Italiana Marchio 2015. Serves 2.

Ingredients

180g Carnaroli rice

2 heaped tbsp Sencha green tea mixture

Peel from ½ lemon, finely chopped

1 tsp shallots, finely chopped

Good fruity extra virgin olive oil (we use Colline Pontine DOP Paola Orsini organic)

100g fresh Morecambe Bay shrimps

Table salt, to taste

Method

Put the tea infusion in 500ml of almost boiling water for 4 minutes.

In a large pan, fry the shallots with a large spoon of extra virgin olive oil over low heat, adding a little drop of tea to prevent burning. The shallots need to become transparent and soft to disappear completely into the risotto.

Add the rice, and toast it well. Cook gradually, adding the green tea a little at a time and allowing it to be absorbed by the rice before adding more, as you normally would with stock.

Cook for about 12 minutes, then add the Morecambe Bay shrimps and lemon peel.

Adjust the seasoning and leave to cook for another 3 minutes.

Remove from the heat and stir in a large spoon of extra virgin olive oil before serving.

Hospitality ACTION

Hospitality Action is the trade charity offering a crucial lifeline to people of all ages, working and retired, from the hospitality industry.

Whether they are approached by a chef, housekeeper, school cook or waiter, Hospitality Action will endeavour to support, whatever the difficulty.

Sometimes all it takes is a very small change in circumstances to tip the balance and turn a manageable situation into an unmanageable one. An extended illness, such as cancer, can lead to a sudden and unexpected drop in pay, whilst a relationship breakdown, bereavement or redundancy, can also put a strain on the household budget.

The charity strives to keep their support relevant to the industry and helps financially when required. Those at the start of their career are educated on the dangers of alcohol and drug misuse via a series of popular seminars. Those currently working can receive support via the Hospitality Action Employee Assistance Programme, 24 hours a day, 365 days per year, whilst industry retirees are welcome to join their very popular befriending scheme to help prevent loneliness and isolation.

The charity recently launched a brand new hard-hitting advertising campaign. The adverts feature images of five of the UK's most renowned chefs having fallen on hard times and aims to raise awareness of the charity and of the issues that can affect hospitality workers both past and present.

The UK-wide campaign depicts Hospitality Action Patron and Trustee Jason Atherton struggling with an addiction, Angela Hartnett illustrated as a victim of domestic violence, Tom Kerridge portrayed as someone suffering from a critical illness, Heston Blumenthal Principal Patron of Hospitality Action portrayed as suffering a serious injury and Ashley Palmer-Watts shown as a sufferer of depression.

The campaign will act as a startling reminder that these things can happen to anyone. Emma Astwood and Edna Bradshaw are just two people who have been helped by Hospitality Action, and we take a look at their stories here.

Domestic violence

Depression

Critical illness

Addiction

Emma Astwood,
Housekeeper

Emma and her son moved to the north leaving a troubled past behind them. Happy in her job as a housekeeper Emma was devastated when she was diagnosed with breast cancer. Needing both chemotherapy and radiotherapy, she was forced to leave work and face the uncertain future. Struggling to come to terms with her diagnosis, Emma worried she was becoming a burden on her family. Her many hospital visits added to her financial outgoings and her utility bills increased as she became more heat sensitive as a consequence of her treatment. No longer able to afford the rental on her washer/dryer Emma turned to Hospitality Action. We helped to buy a replacement enabling Emma to focus on her son, on her health and to become a little more self-reliant.

Edna Bradshaw,
Barmaid

Edna worked as a barmaid for over a decade. Now in her seventies, Edna suffers from painful chronic osteoporosis of the hip and spine. Her husband John has been diagnosed with prostate cancer and has sadly also undergone surgery for bowel cancer. Both Edna and John have mobility problems and really feel the cold, but with no savings to call upon, the couple found themselves unable to install central heating in their home. They relied only on a gas fire in the living room and their cooker for warmth. Edna and John contacted Hospitality Action and we were able to provide the couple with a grant towards the cost of installing a gas boiler and radiators helping to keep them warm over the winter.

John said: "The central heating has made a tremendous difference to our lives."

Hospitality Action receives no government funding and so is dependent on individuals and corporate bodies from within the hospitality industry to support its vital work.

If you would like to make a donation to Hospitality Action simply text Chef16 £5 to 70070

For more information and ways to support please contact:
Dawn Holding via dawn@dawnholding.co.uk
Visit: www.hospitalityaction.org.uk
Twitter: @HospActionNorth
Facebook: HospitalityAction
Registered Charity No: 1101083

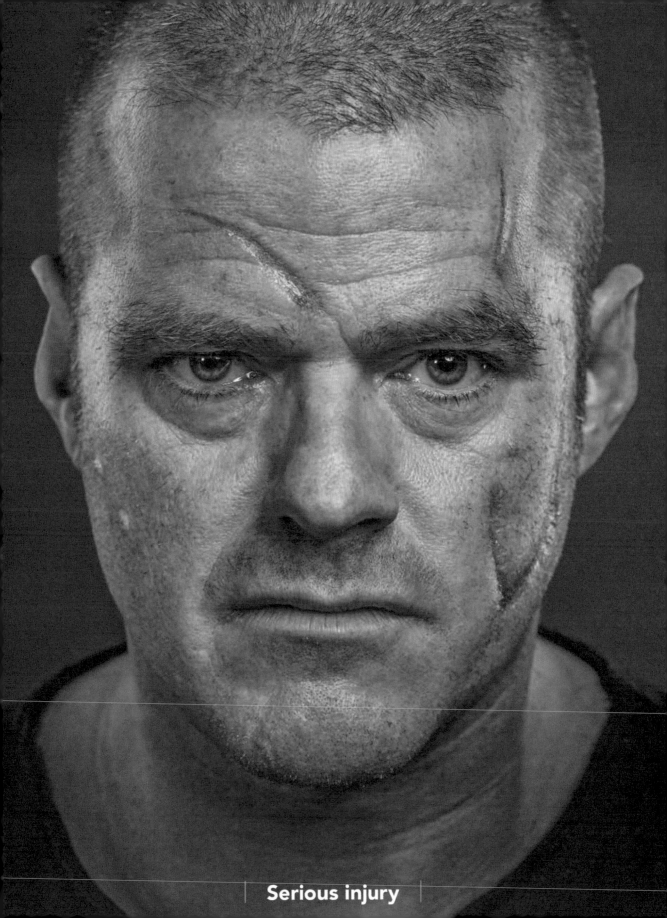

Serious injury

Home produced and HAND PICKED

On the cusp of Lancashire, West Yorkshire and Great Manchester, Albion Farm Shop sells the best of local produce from the three counties

Albion Farm, Saddleworth, has been in the Hirst family for more than a century, but the farm shop and its award-winning café are more recent additions.

Laura Hirst said: "It was a poultry farm originally, and my dad, David, and grandad Sidney, introduced pedigree Welsh Black cattle and then Annette introduced the pedigree polled Dorset Horn sheep. They used to sell our own meat and eggs from the door, and we had an honesty box in the porch outside."

The idea for the farm shop came after numerous farming difficulties, including epidemics of foot and mouth disease and mad cow disease, none of which directly affected Albion Farm, but knocked the farming industry.

The shop itself didn't actually open until 2008, after Annette and David realised that something more had to be done. Located on the border of Lancashire, West Yorkshire and Greater Manchester, it regularly pulls in customers from across a wide area, attracted by the produce from Albion Farm itself and surrounding producers who have been hand-picked for quality.

"I get out as much as I can to farmers' markets and source lots of things directly. It's important to taste and feel it for yourself," said Laura.

"The meat is excellent quality, not just our own, but we also have free-range pork, which we use for our homemade sausages and hog roasts, free-range chicken and game, all locally sourced. We have lots of homemade produce on the deli, such as pies, Scotch eggs, home cooked meats, and sandwich fillings for our made to order take away sandwiches.

"We have a British cheese counter with lots of tasty cheeses as well as a shop full of jams, biscuits, cakes, snacks, fruit, veg, spirits, ales and much more!"

The adjoining café provides a large homemade menu, including award-winning farm shop breakfasts, made with ingredients from the butchery counter, to full home cooked meals and proper puddings, sandwiches, cakes and Lilian's afternoon tea, which is named after Grandma Lilian Hirst who is 95 and still loving her food.

Their newest addition is their 'Drive-Thru' hog roast, which is located on their bottom car park every Friday and Sunday lunch time, and serves up delicious free-range pork sandwiches which have become a huge hit!

Little Saddleworth
Pork Pie
£2.60

Little Saddleworth
Cheese, Leek
+ onion pie
£2.60

Little Saddleworth
Pork + Chi
Pie

Albion Farm Shop
CHEESE AND ONION PIE

Packed with the flavour of mature cheddar, this is a prince among pies.

Serves 6-8.

Ingredients

For the pastry:

800g plain flour

400g butter, cubed and softened

5-6 tbsp cold water

Pinch of salt and pepper

1 egg, beaten (for egg wash)

For the filling:

500g quality farmhouse mature cheddar (we use two from our deli), grated

150g mashed potato (no cream or butter)

4 large onions, finely chopped

2 tbsp plain flour

50ml double cream

1 tbsp English mustard

Oil

Pinch of salt and pepper

Method

For the pastry

Sift the flour into a bowl, add the butter and rub together using your fingertips until the mixture resembles breadcrumbs. Slowly add small amounts of the water until the mix comes together to form a dough. Wrap in cling film and leave to rest in the fridge for 1 hour.

For the filling

Bring a medium-sized saucepan up to medium heat, and gently soften the onions in oil for around 5-10 minutes, depending on how much crunch you like. When the onions are soft, add the flour, mashed potato, double cream, grated cheese and mustard. Cook the flour out for 3-4 minutes, stir well and season to taste with salt and pepper.

Preheat the oven to 180°C. Grease a deep 20cm/8in pie tin.

When the pastry has chilled, roll out two-thirds on a clean, floured work surface until it is almost twice as wide as the diameter of the pie tin.

Using the rolling pin, lift the pastry and lay it over the pie tin to line the base and sides.

Gently press the pastry into the corners of the tin, trimming off any excess, then prick the base of the pastry case several times with a fork.

To assemble

Once the pie filling has cooled, pour into the pastry lined pie tin and compress down until it is level with the top of the tin.

Roll the remaining one-third of the pastry out onto a clean, floured work surface until it is slightly larger than the diameter of the pie tin. Brush the rim of the pastry case with some of the beaten egg and place the pastry lid on top of the pie. Trim off any excess pastry. Seal the pastry lid to the pastry case by crimping the edges with a fork.

With a knife, make two small holes in the centre of the pastry lid to allow steam to escape while cooking. Brush the pastry lid with the remaining beaten egg, then transfer to the oven and bake for 35-40 minutes, or until golden brown.

*This is not our exact shop recipe, as that is top secret, but this is almost, equally as delicious!

Albion Farm Shop
RAG PUDDING

A traditional Lancashire favourite made using steak, real ale and wonderfully indulgent suet pastry. Serves 4.

Ingredients

For the suet pastry:

400g plain flour

200g shredded beef suet

Small amount of cold water

1 egg, beaten (to use as a wash on the pastry)

For the filling:

1kg top quality braising steak, diced

500ml real ale (we use Black Sheep)

1 large onion, finely chopped

2 large carrots, chopped into small cubes

3 sticks celery, finely chopped

2 leeks, finely chopped

4 cloves garlic, crushed

1 sprig each of rosemary and thyme

1 bay leaf

Good quality beef stock (or use 4 stock cubes)

Cooking oil

Method

For the pastry

Add the flour and beef suet to a mixing bowl, mix well and slowly add the water a little at a time. Start to bring the mixture together with your hands until it forms a smooth elastic dough. It is worth bearing in mind that suet pastry takes in a lot more water than other pastry, so if the mix feels a little dry, keep adding a few drops of water.

For the filling

Heat a small amount of oil in a large pan and add the vegetables and garlic. Slightly brown all the vegetables for around 10 minutes, then add the braising steak. Keep stirring the vegetables and the beef until all the meat is seared.

Add the ale, herbs, bay leaf and enough beef stock to cover the mixture, topping up with water if necessary. Bring to the boil, then turn the heat right down and simmer for 3 hours.

To assemble

The mix should be completely chilled before assembly, preferably overnight.

Take the suet pastry and divide into 4 pieces and roll into balls. Sprinkle flour on to a clean smooth work surface and roll the pastry out to the thickness of a one pound coin.

Take a large serving spoon of the steak mixture and add to the centre of the suet pastry, then take a small amount of egg wash and brush around the steak mix. Fold the sides of the pastry over the mix, then egg wash the sides again and fold the remaining pastry over the mix.

Put a sheet of cling film onto a smooth surface and put the rag pudding at one end, then roll up as tightly as possible in the cling film. Repeat the process with tin foil, and leave to rest in the fridge for 30 minutes before cooking.

You can choose to poach in water or steam. Poaching takes around 40 minutes in simmering water, steaming will take 50-60 minutes.

Locally GROWN

A farm shop that's a cook's delight, plus a restaurant and café majoring in Lancashire flavours gives Barton Grange Garden Centre some real foodie credentials.

With a heritage dating back to the 1960s and a new site that opened in 2008, Barton Grange Garden Centre is justifiably proud of its deep Lancashire roots.

The centre, part of the family-owned Barton Grange Group, has won the industry's Destination Garden Centre of the Year title for five consecutive years. The award is judged on everything from car parking to food – and the food is a key ingredient in Barton Grange's great reputation.

Home to a farm shop, Willows Restaurant and Riverside Café visitors are certainly well-fed. The farm shop prides itself on stocking everything you could need for a recipe, with key ingredients sourced from Lancashire, the UK and beyond.

Barton Grange's Kate Ford said: "We sometimes sell herbs, salad, raspberries, strawberries and asparagus from our own nursery.

"Most of the suppliers are hand-picked – we've been out to see them and we're proud to champion them.

"We are lucky to have so many brilliant cheese producers right on our doorstep such as Grandma Singletons, Sandham's and Dewlay who produce the Garstang Blue that was used by Jamie Oliver."

The butchery counter is run by Honeywell's, which sells locally reared meat, and other mouth-watering local goodies include yoghurts, preserves, ice cream, pies and superb Lancashire cheesecakes.

"These are all people very close to us," says Kate.

"But there is a real mix in there, such as really, really top quality olive oil. It's an absolute joy shopping for food in the farm shop."

Many of the ingredients that can be bought in the farm shop are found in dishes cooked in the restaurant, such as pear and Garstang blue cheese tartlet, confit Goosnargh duckling and Brock Valley steak and ale pie all make the most of local ingredients. The menus change every few months to use produce at its seasonal best.

"A lot of customers are very proud of our food heritage and like the fact we use local produce," said Kate.

"Many come to the garden centre and just happen to pop into Willows or the Riverside for lunch, but then they come back because they like the food. And there are some customers who come just for the food!"

Barton Grange
LANCASTER LEMON TART

A delicious tea-time treat combining a sweet pastry with the refreshing, zesty flavour of lemons. Serves 8-10.

Ingredients

For the sweet pastry:

227g plain flour

113g margarine

56g caster sugar

28g beaten egg

For the filling:

100g lemon curd

113g butter, softened

85g caster sugar

2 large eggs, beaten

113g self-raising flour

28g ground almonds

1½ lemons, zest and juice only

28g flaked almonds

Method

For the sweet pastry

Use your fingertips to rub together the flour and margarine to make a crumb mixture.

Mix together the egg and sugar, add it to the bowl and mix in to form a dough. Leave to rest in the fridge for 10-15 minutes. Preheat the oven to 200°C.

Roll out the pastry to line a flan tin. Spread the lemon curd over the pastry.

For the filling

Cream together the butter and sugar until light and fluffy. Add the beaten eggs gradually and mix well.

Carefully fold in the flour and ground almonds, then fold in the lemon zest and juice. Spread the mixture over the lemon curd and sprinkle with flaked almonds.

Pop in the oven at 200°C for 15 minutes then reduce the heat to 150°C and continue to bake for 25-30 minutes.

Serve warm or cold with custard, cream or yoghurt.

Homemade HEAVEN

From its roots as an old dairy building to a destination venue for foodies and couples tying the knot, Bashall Barn is a trailblazer off the beaten track.

Bashall Barn started off in 2001 as a small rural farm shop in unused buildings belonging to the family's Ribble Valley dairy farm and has been growing and diversifying ever since, expanding to include an award-winning restaurant, coffee shop, ice cream parlour and now wedding venue.

Managing Director Simon Barnes, who sold air conditioning to Nissan in his previous life, said: "It was a pure coincidence the buildings became available just as I wanted to come back home to the farm.

"My brother does the farming side, and I am glad to say the two separate businesses continue all these years later, with Bashall Barn growing as a destination venue at the heart of the valley, a few miles off the A59."

The same homemade produce crafted in the kitchen is sold in the shop, throughout the catering business and now served to wedding guests.

Simon said: "The same amazing quality of ice cream that we put in a tub for the farm shop, goes onto a cone in the ice cream parlour and a scoop in a beautiful dessert for a wedding.

"We use a local greengrocer, butcher and fishmonger and then we convert this local produce into a finished product.

"Nothing is mass-produced or bought in. If you have a pâté starter, you can come back and buy the same thing in the farm shop.

"It's exactly the same product, which is unusual. Where we can it is locally sourced and home-produced." The restaurant specialises in traditional Lancastrian dishes, with seasonal elements and specials. Diners range from "the person across the road to Australian visitors," said Simon.

He added: "We are very lucky to have such a loyal, local customer base, linked to this is the stunningly beautiful local area, we are very lucky to live and work here."

"Our catering started with a kettle and me making ginger cake in an old oven, now we cater for evening wedding parties of up to 200 people" said Simon.

"We've come a long way and are constantly evolving and I think that is why customers keep coming back – they like to be part of a continuing local success story."

Bashall Barn Farm Shop

Bashall Barn
BRAISED BLADE OF BEEF

A hearty, melt in the mouth braised steak dish in a flavoursome red wine sauce.
Serves 4.

Ingredients

4 beef blade steaks

2 carrots, diced

4 celery sticks, diced

½ swede, diced

1 large onion, diced

1 litre beef stock (approx)

200ml red wine

4 sprigs fresh thyme, chopped

2 bay leaves

Salt and pepper

Olive oil

Mashed potato

Pea shoots

Method

Seal off the blades of beef in a little oil in a frying pan, then place in a roasting tray. Season with salt and pepper.

Dice all the vegetables to roughly same size, then fry off in the same pan as the blades of beef. Once browned, add them to the roasting tray with the blades of beef.

Deglaze the frying pan by adding red wine, reduce by half, then add the stock. Once simmering, pour over the beef and vegetables in the roasting tray, just to cover.

Add the thyme and bay leaves, then cover the tray with foil.

Braise in the oven for 2½ hours at 150°C until the blades are really tender.

Once cooked, take out the blades, strain out the vegetables and set aside. Thicken the cooking liquor by reducing it (add cornflour to thicken if necessary). Pop the beef and vegetables back into the tray with the sauce.

Serve on top of mashed potato, garnished with fresh pea shoots. We enjoy this recipe with a glass of merlot.

Be Chocolate
CRÈME FRAÎCHE MOUSSE
WITH SPICED MANGO PURÉE

A totally tropical taste for this fresh and zingy layered pudding with a surprise mango jelly centre. Serves 6.

Ingredients

For the coconut base:

100g icing sugar syrup

50g coconut

30g plain flour

75g egg whites (approximately 2 eggs)

75g butter

For the crème fraîche mousse:

50g invert sugar syrup

50g sugar

30g water

75g egg yolks, whisked (approximately 4 eggs)

40g whipping cream

8g gelatine

340g semi-whipped cream

375g crème fraîche

1 vanilla pod

For the mango jelly insert:

100g mango purée

1g agar agar

For the spiced mango purée:

2 limes, zested and juiced

20g ginger

250g mango purée

50ml stock syrup

3g agar agar

Method

For the coconut base

Place the icing sugar, coconut and flour into a bowl.

Melt the butter and add to the egg whites, then mix well into the flour, coconut and icing sugar, making sure there are no lumps.

Spread evenly onto a lined baking sheet and bake 175°C until golden brown. Remove from the oven and leave to cool in the tray.

For the crème fraîche mousse

Make a classic sabayon by boiling the sugars in the water and add in to the whisked egg yolks. Warm the first amount of cream to 80°C and dissolve the gelatine in it. Pour this onto the whisked yolks.

Fold in the semi-whipped cream, vanilla and crème fraîche. Pour the mix into your chosen moulds.

For the mango jelly insert

Warm the purée and add the agar agar. Bring up to the boil, then leave to set. Cut out into your desired shapes and place a piece in the centre of each mould, so it is encased in the mousse.

For the spiced mango purée

Place the stock syrup, purée, lime zest, juice and ginger into a pan and bring up to the boil. Leave to infuse.

Add the agar agar to the mix and bring back up to the boil. Pass through a fine sieve.

To assemble and serve

Cut the coconut base into pieces to fit the top of the moulds, then invert and un-mould so the coconut base is at the bottom. Serve garnished with the spiced mango purée.

Destination DINING

Culinary excellence combined with fantastic views - and an adult-only dining experience - helps create Bertram's Restaurant's unique ambience.

Bertram's Restaurant is a destination restaurant set within the award-winning Woodland Spa which opened in 2013 following a £4.5million investment.

Now it is rapidly becoming recognised as one of the North West's culinary and social destinations.

The restaurant is unique, stylish and contemporary. Set in an elevated position and accessed via its own lift, Bertram's boasts breathtaking views over Pendle Hill and the surrounding 100 acres of greenbelt countryside.

By day, the restaurant attracts a variety of guests from spa visitors who dine from a varied menu as part of their spa day dining experience and business lunch clientele, to those enjoying the quintessential yet unparalleled afternoon tea experience.

In the evening it morphs into something quite different. The restaurant is cultured, cosmopolitan and becomes the 'see and be seen' destination of choice where guests enjoy an affordable yet exceptional adult-only dining experience.

"There's a vibrant atmosphere, a more sophisticated evening where people can truly relax away from life's restrictions and routines and choose from an expansive wine and cocktail list whilst enjoying live weekend music. It's not a stuffy, fine dining experience. But it is an experience not to be missed." Said head chef Spencer Burge.

"My food philosophy for Bertram's is simple: consistency is the key."

The imaginative menus focus on regionally-sourced produce wherever possible, including a noteworthy Lancashire cheeseboard and locally-reared meat.

Bertram's has a character and identity of its own – from the subtle but sophisticated styling, to the culinary excellence.

Bertram's
RESTAURANT

Bertram's Restaurant
LEMON AND BUTTERMILK SCONES

Light and zesty lemon scone perfection made simple using a food processor.
Makes 8-10.

Ingredients

250g superfine 00 plain flour, sifted

50g plain flour, sifted

24g baking powder

1g salt

75g butter, chilled and small diced

90g buttermilk

2 lemons, zest only

1 large egg, lightly beaten

60g caster sugar

2 egg yolks, lightly beaten for glazing

Method

Mix together the flour, baking powder, salt and sugar in a food mixer with the dough hook, then add the butter and bring to a breadcrumb like consistency.

Add the lemon zest and buttermilk to the egg, then pour into the dry ingredients. Start the machine on low speed, stopping at intervals to help the flour incorporate. Do not over work.

Wrap the dough in cling film and rest for 30 minutes.

Once rested, roll out to approximately 2cm thick and cut out with a 2 ½ in (6.35cm) cutter, making sure you flour your cutter after every cut. Do not twist.

Place each scone on a greaseproof papered tray and brush the top with the beaten egg yolks. Allow to dry and repeat the egg wash. Try not to let the egg wash drip down the sides as this will hinder the rising of the scone.

Cook in a preheated oven for 10 minutes at 200°C.

Bertram's Restaurant
SESAME SALMON YAKISOBA

Bertram's version of this Japanese classic brings together salmon with colourful vegetables, noodles and an aromatic sauce. Serves 6.

Ingredients

4x 150g salmon pieces, skin on

For the stir-fry

½ red pepper, deseeded and thinly sliced

½ yellow pepper, deseeded and thinly sliced

100g mangetout, sliced in half

2 spring onions, thinly sliced

1 small red onion, thinly sliced

2 cloves garlic, finely chopped

1 head broccoli, cut into small florets

360g soba noodles

1 tbsp sesame oil

Salt and pepper

Toasted sesame seeds

Olive oil, for frying

For the sauce

100ml teriyaki sauce

40ml crushed yellow bean sauce

2 sticks lemongrass, finely chopped

1 tbsp fresh ginger, peeled and grated

½ red chilli, deseeded

1 tbsp light soy sauce

Method

For the sauce

Put all the sauce ingredients into a food blender and blitz until smooth.

For the salmon

Heat olive oil in a large non-stick pan over high heat. Liberally season the salmon pieces, then place skin side down in the pan and reduce the heat to medium-low. Do not move the fillets.

Cook for about 7 minutes or until well browned and cooked around three-quarters of the way through. Turn the fillets and cook for around a further 3 minutes, or until still just barely pink in the centre. Brush with sesame oil.

For the stir-fry

Cook the broccoli in a large pan of boiling salted water for 2-3 minutes until just tender, drain thoroughly and refresh under cold water. Repeat the process with the noodles.

Heat a wok over a medium heat for 1-2 minutes until hot and almost smoking, then add the olive oil, peppers and onions. After 30 seconds, add the garlic, 30 seconds later, add rest of vegetables and then the cooked noodles. Stir-fry for 1 minute then pour enough sauce over the noodles to coat both the noodles and the vegetables and bring to the boil.

To serve

Arrange the noodles in a bowl, sprinkle with toasted sesame seeds and place the cooked salmon on top.

You can use any variation of noodles or vegetables with this recipe. It's nice garnished with pickled ginger.

Bertram's Restaurant
PISTACHIO AND WHITE CHOCOLATE BROWNIE

Melding the richness of two types of chocolate with the crunch of pistachios
into a truly indulgent brownie. Makes 8.

Ingredients

200g dark chocolate (54% cocoa)

170g unsalted butter

2 eggs

70g plain flour

120g toasted pistachio nuts

200g dark brown sugar

1 tsp baking powder

1 tsp vanilla extract

120g white chocolate buttons

Method

Melt the butter and dark chocolate slowly over a bain-marie, then allow to cool slightly.

Whisk the eggs, sugar and vanilla until light, pale and fluffy, then stir in the warm chocolate mixture.

Stir in the flour, baking powder, nuts and white chocolate buttons until evenly incorporated.

Spread evenly into an 8 x 9 inch baking tray lined with grease proof paper and bake at 165°C for 20-25 minutes.

Allow to cool and cut into eight slices.

Perfect PUB GRUB

The latest Nutter venture, The Bird at Birtle, takes pub food to a new level with Lancashire ingredients sprinkled with the celebrity chef's signature style.

"My dad came in and said 'Merry Christmas, I've just bought you a pub,'" says Andrew Nutter.

His new venture, The Bird at Birtle has transformed the former Bird I'Th Hand pub at Birtle into a gastropub serving up regional produce with the Nutter twist, plus cask ales.

Andrew said: "It's a different format to Nutters. We've kept the pubby feel of things downstairs so people can meet up with their mates and linger by the bar, then they can meander up the stairway and take in the atmosphere and the fabulous food."

The kitchen is headed by Carl Tait who previously worked at Nutters for 18 years and front of house by Hannah Powell who is another one of Nutters protégés.

He describes the flavour of The Bird at Birtle as "Lancashire fare with flair and imagination," that keeps the core elements of the much-loved Nutters menu but offers a more informal and casual dining experience. The signature Nutters Bury black pudding wontons dish has been turned into a bar snack.

The new venue shares similar great views across the Lancashire countryside to its big sister restaurant thanks to the floor to ceiling glass at the rear of the dining area and a glass terrace.

"We've knocked the building around a bit," says Andrew.

It's not just the fabric of the pub that has been knocked around. The whole taste of The Bird has changed from its former incarnation.

Andrew said: "It was a pub before that was renowned for doing classics like cheese and onion pie and mixed grill. We're giving people a bit more and taking it to the next level with products that people will come back for, pushing the boundaries with the impact of flavour."

The son of a Lancashire butcher and a home economics teacher, Andrew may have cooked around the world, but his heart is in his home county.

He believes Lancashire food is so great because of the "sheer passion" of the producers.

"Whether that's local cheese makers or ducks, chicken and turkeys running around, producers have passion and enthusiasm for what they're doing," he says.

"We're taking people on a journey at The Bird at Birtle and we want to create that same passion about what they're putting in their mouths."

The Bird at Birtle

The Bird at Birtle

BRILL, WILD GARLIC PESTO, FORMBY ASPARGUS, FERMENTED BLACK GARLIC AND LEMON DRESSING

"A dish that showcases the finest of Lancashire produce. Simplicity is the key element letting the quality of the local ingredients shine." Andrew Nutter. Serves 4.

Ingredients

4 x 140g fillets of brill, skinned

2 tbsp olive oil

For the wild garlic pesto:

100g wild garlic

30g toasted cashew nuts

50g Parmesan cheese, grated

100ml olive oil

For the black garlic dressing:

50g black garlic (available online if you can't find it locally)

1 lemon, juice and zest

100ml olive oil

To serve:

1 bunch Formby asparagus, blanched

Heritage tomatoes

Mixed leaves

Method

For the wild garlic pesto

Take the wild garlic, cashew nuts, Parmesan and olive oil and blend to a smooth paste. Season.

For the black garlic dressing

Take the black garlic, lemon juice, zest and olive oil and blend to a smooth purée. Season.

For the fish

Heat a non-stick pan until hot, add the olive oil and seal the fish for about 2-3 minutes until golden. Turn over, and cook for a further minute.

Place the fish on a tray, add a spoonful of the wild garlic pesto and place under a hot grill for a minute.

To serve

When ready to serve, arrange the asparagus, tomatoes and mixed leaves on serving plates.

Take the black garlic dressing and drizzle over the salad, adding the fish to the top and finally a squeeze of lemon to finish.

Canalside CLASSICS

The Blue Mallard Restaurant serves up casual fine dining and hugely popular theme nights, with canalside views from a redeveloped stable block at Burscough Wharf.

Based in what was once stables housing the horses that pulled barges along the Leeds-Liverpool canal, The Blue Mallard takes its name from the ducks that diners can see through the 8ft waterside windows at the front of the restaurant.

Owner, head chef and local lad, Chris Crowell opened the restaurant in 2011, moving into a venue that had stood derelict for years before being redeveloped. Today, the first-floor restaurant still shows signs of its heritage with the high ceilings and original beams that are complemented by wooden floors and tables.

"I'm from Burscough originally, I grew up here and travelled around, and was lucky to work with some really good chefs," says Chris.

"I brought back what I learned to Burscough and opened up The Mallard."

The local flavour isn't confined to Chris; Lancashire ingredients are central to the contemporary British casual fine dining the restaurant serves up.

"That's the approach we decided to take when we opened, with a focus on local products and suppliers," says Chris.

"It began with a farm shop a mile down the road. They grow a lot of their own stuff and we get it all muddy and wet, straight out of the field that morning."

You'll find the local parsnips alongside local duck – but not those in the canal – on the menu, along with fish from Fleetwood, locally-reared meat, Brown's black pudding, Mrs Dowsons ice cream and bread from the Lancashire Bread House in Burscough.

The Blue Mallard also serves up tasting menus and monthly theme nights, ranging from Spanish, Greek and Italian to cuisine from a little closer to home.

"A couple of times, we've done a Lancashire night, with a themed menu on local Lancashire produce, and dishes with our own little twist," said Chris.

"One of the dishes is a tasting of Causeway Farm vegetables done in lots of different ways. People know Causeway Farm and really like what we're doing.

"We're seeing a shift. People are more aware about what's in the food they're eating, where it's come from and where it's grown."

The Blue Mallard

The Blue Mallard

SMOKED COD WITH SOUTHPORT SHRIMP SOUFFLE, BUTTERED KALE, MRS KIRKHAM'S LANCASHIRE CHEESE AND LEEK CROQUETTES WITH WATERCRESS SAUCE

A Lancashire delight made from The Blue Mallard's own smoked cod, shrimps from James Peet, cream from Rowland's Dairy and kale and potatoes from Causeway Farm, watercress from Duerden Brothers and leeks grown in Burscough. Serves 4.

Ingredients

4 x 250g smoked cod fillets

1 pint milk

1 large bunch kale

Large knob of butter

For the Lancashire cheese and leek croquettes:

500g Maris Piper potatoes

100g Mrs Kirkham's Lancashire cheese

1 leek, split, washed and finely chopped

Knob of butter

Pinch chopped chives

Salt and pepper

Flour for pane

2 eggs for eggwash

Breadcrumbs for pane

For the Southport shrimp soufflé:

50g butter

40g plain flour

220ml semi skimmed milk

4 medium free-range eggs, separated

80g Southport shrimps

Pinch parsley, chopped

For the watercress sauce:

40ml dry white wine

1 shallot, peeled and fine diced

1 bay leaf

300ml double cream

1 bunch watercress

Sea salt

Method

For the croquettes

In a large pan of salted water, cook the potatoes until starting to crumble, then drain and mash with butter, salt and pepper. Gently soften the leeks in butter, but don't colour.

While the mash is still warm, crumble in the cheese, leeks and chives and season. Shape into 10cm long sausage shapes and chill.

When chilled, gently coat in flour, egg wash, then roll in breadcrumbs. Either cook in a deep fat fryer at 180°C for 4-5 minutes and finish in the oven at 180°C for 4-5 minutes, or shallow fry until the breadcrumbs are golden brown, then pop in the oven for 10-15 minutes.

For the watercress sauce

Add the wine, shallot and bay leaf to a heavy bottomed saucepan on a medium heat. Reduce by half. Add the cream and reduce by two-thirds. Remove the bay leaf, add the watercress and blend with a hand blender for 1 minute. Pass through a fine sieve, season with sea salt and set aside.

For the soufflé

Butter 4 large ramekins and put in a roasting tin. In a heavy bottomed saucepan, melt the butter then whisk in the flour to a smooth paste. Slowly whisk in the milk and on a low heat, cook out until it thickens to a smooth sauce and doesn't taste floury.

Remove from the heat and whisk in the egg yolks, parsley and shrimp. Season with salt.

In a large bowl, whisk the egg whites to a soft peak – when the whisk is pulled out the top flops down – and fold in the shrimp mix, keeping as much air in the mix as possible. Spoon evenly into the ramekins.

Fill the roasting tray with boiling water to halfway up the outside of the ramekins and bake in a preheated oven at 200°C for 20 minutes. Don't open the oven too early or the soufflés will sink.

For the cod

Poached in a mix of lightly seasoned half milk and half water on a low heat for 6-8 minutes. Remove the cod with a slotted spoon and drain on kitchen paper.

Cook the kale in a large pan of salted water on a rolling boil for 1 minute. Drain, season and add a good-sized knob of butter.

To serve

Sit the cod on a bed of kale, with croquettes and soufflé on the side and a generous amount of watercress sauce.

The Blue Mallard

MELTING CHOCOLATE FONDANT WITH WHITE CHOCOLATE AND HONEYCOMB PARFAIT

A mixture of sumptuous tastes and textures come together in a sublime sweet made with milk and cream sourced from Rowland's Dairy and Chocolate Magic's chocolate, both based in Mawdesley. Serves 6.

Ingredients

Ingredients

For the melting chocolate:

230g dark chocolate, 54% or above

180g caster sugar

6 medium eggs

90g plain flour, sieved

180g unsalted butter, cut into 1cm dice

For the honeycomb:

400g caster sugar

100ml runny honey

2 tbsp liquid glucose

1½ tsp bicarbonate of soda

(Divide in two between the parfait and garnish)

For the white chocolate and honeycomb parfait:

50ml cold water

4 egg yolks

80g caster sugar

120g grated white chocolate

Smashed up honeycomb

400ml double cream

Method

Preheat the oven to 180°C.

For the honeycomb

Put the sugar, honey and glucose in a heavy based saucepan with 100ml of water. Place the pan on the heat and, using a sugar thermometer, bring to the boil and boil at 160°C.

Grease a large baking tray with oil while the sugar is boiling. When the pan reaches the required temperature, remove from the heat, quickly add the bicarb and whisk speedily.

Working quickly, pour the mixture on to the tray - it will start to bubble dramatically straight away – and leave to cool.

For the white chocolate and honeycomb parfait

In a large heatproof bowl (preferably stainless steel) over a pan of simmering water, whisk together the egg yolks, sugar and water for about 4-5 minutes until the mixture is light in colour, thick and fluffy.

Remove the bowl from the pan and stir in the grated chocolate, then set aside to cool slightly. Whilst this is cooling, whisk the cream to soft peaks.

When the chocolate mix has cooled, fold the cream into it and add the smashed up honeycomb.

Put into the freezer and stir occasionally. You can either set in a mould to slice or serve with an ice cream scoop.

For the melting chocolate fondant

Melt the chocolate and butter together in a heatproof bowl over a pan of simmering water, stirring regularly to prevent splitting.

In a large bowl, whisk together the egg yolks and sugar for about 4-5 minutes until pale and fluffy in texture (cold sabayon).

When the chocolate and butter have melted, remove from the heat and allow to cool slightly for 5 minutes.

Slowly add the chocolate to the egg and sugar mix, then fold in the sieved flour. Make sure all ingredients are combined without any lumps.

Take 6 medium sized ramekins and spoon in the mixture to just below the rim. Bake in the preheated oven for 10-12 minutes until the top cracks slightly.

Serve immediately with the parfait and extra honeycomb for garnish.

Quality mix of traditional AND MODERN

Family-run Brown's the Butchers specialise in local meat, new and traditional recipes and their famous English haggis.

"In the 1930s and 40s, we brought live cattle on the train from farms and auctions, unloaded them at the railway station, and walked them through the main street in Chorley," says John Brown, whose family started Brown's the Butchers in 1932.

"This particular young bull had gone a bit mad and lost its blindfold. I said to my dad: 'We'll never get it through town', but he went into the parcel office, got some strong twine and tied it round the ring in its nose and then around its testicles. It walked along as quiet as a lamb."

There have been some radical changes since John began at the business aged 11, sorting ration book tickets after school. Today, the fourth generation – John's sons Tim and Chris – man the decks, but Tim says his father "steers the ship".

"Dad is 77 and is one of fewer than 100 Master Butchers left in the country," says Tim.

"We're very fortunate to have his knowledge around us. He's still working six days a week."

John began making the Lancashire haggis for which the shop is famous, and Tim, a qualified chef, insists that Lancashire rather than Scotland has a big claim to being home of the delicacy.

"The first written recipe for haggis was in the early 1400s in a book written in the Lancashire dialect," he says.

"We've found a lot of things in old recipes. Dad was rooting around in the attic and he found an old black pudding recipe scratched on a piece of paper.

"We thought we'd have a go and we now make award-winning Lancashire Farmhouse black pudding loaf. It's baked in a block and the taste is unbelievable."

The majority of Browns' lamb and pork is sourced locally and beef is supplied direct from a farm in the Lake District. Brown's also has its own drying room, producing continental-style charcuterie.

"When you know where it comes from and how it was reared, you can stand behind it 100 per cent," says Tim.

"We like to see customers as friends not just a number. We sell tailored meats, for individual needs, not plastic packets."

Brown's the Butchers

BRAISED HAGGIS STUFFED PORK BELLY

A hearty meaty indulgence served with honey and cumin roast root vegetables, dauphinoise potatoes and creamed leeks. Serves 6.

Ingredients

For the pork and roast vegetables:

1kg belly pork, deboned, butterflied and stuffed with haggis (your butcher can do this for you)

A selection of carrots, parsnips, swede and celeriac

Honey

Cumin seeds

Olive oil

Salt and pepper

For the dauphinoise potatoes:

1kg waxy potatoes

250ml double cream

1 clove garlic, peeled and halved

For the creamed leeks:

6 leeks

500ml double cream

50ml white wine

For the pork loin and black pudding:

500g pork loin, sliced

350g black pudding, sliced

150g self-raising flour

180ml sparkling water

Method

For the pork and roast vegetables

Cover the belly pork with foil and cook for 4-5 hours at 140°C. Remove the foil and turn up the heat to 200°C for the last 20-25 minutes to crisp the skin.

Peel and dice the root vegetables and blanch in boiling water for 8-10 minutes, or until they are just starting to soften but are not fully cooked. Drain, and toss with the honey, cumin seeds, olive oil and salt and pepper. Roast the vegetables on the same tray as the pork after the foil has been removed, or on a separate tray.

For the dauphinoise potatoes

Preheat the oven to 160°C or 140°C fan. Line a 20cm square tin with greaseproof paper, making sure there are no holes for liquid to seep through. Butter the paper.

Cut the potatoes to the width of a one pound coin and pat dry.

Put the cream into a pan, add the garlic and heat to boiling point then remove. When it has slightly cooled, strain into a jug.

Layer the potatoes in the tin, overlapping slightly, and season with salt and pepper. Pour over half the cream, then layer the rest of the potatoes on top and add the remaining cream.

Bake for 1-1¼ hours until the potatoes are tender and the top is golden. Leave to stand for 5 minutes, then cut into 6 portions to serve.

For the creamed leeks

Split and wash the leeks, then slice thinly. Sweat in a pan with a little olive oil over a low heat for 10-15 minutes then add the white wine and simmer for 5 minutes. Add the cream, simmer for a further 5 minutes then season to taste.

For the pork loin and black pudding

Season the pork loin pieces and seal in a hot pan for 2 minutes on each side. Add a knob of butter and baste for 3 minutes on each side. Remove from the pan and rest for 5 minutes.

Whisk the flour and sparkling water together into a batter. Dip the slices of black pudding in flour, dust off the excess then dip in the batter. Fry for 3 minutes on each side until golden brown.

Recipe supplied by head chef Bruno at The Kitchen Theatre, Chorley. Who proudly use produce supplied by Brown's the Butchers. Bruno is also BBC Radio Lancashire's resident chef.

The Only Bury Black Pudding
ON THE BLOCK

The only Bury black puddings to be made in Bury today, The Bury Black Pudding Company proves that the north west is still making some of the finest black puddings in the UK.

Debbie Pierce began her black pudding story at the age of 12, working as a Saturday girl on Bury Market for James Wallace, a farmer who was one of the longest standing traders on the market. When James retired, Debbie took over the stall, which was supplied with black puddings by Jack and Richard Morris. Jack retired around the same time and his son Richard took over the black pudding production, setting in motion a journey that would see the dedicated pair taking this great northern delicacy from its market stall beginnings to a nationwide operation.

It was Debbie's shrewd business mind that saw the opportunity to expand the flourishing business from its popular market stall. As soon as she saw the emergence of online food websites, she made sure that The Bury Black Pudding Company would be part of this new trend. As a result, she not only increased sales but built awareness of the brand incredibly quickly, getting their products into national supermarkets like Asda, Tesco, Sainsbury's, Morrisons, Waitrose and the Co-op.

Although the highly successful product is now sold through all the big high street supermarkets, the market stall at Bury market is still at the heart and soul of the company. Many long-standing staff have remained employed at the family-run business for years, and the company now employs about 70 people in the Bury area. On the factory floor, the traditional recipe and production methods remain very much the same, providing the hand-finished quality product that the customers know and love.

What is inside these black puddings that has kept them a cut above the competition? As they specialise in making black puddings, you can be assured that only the very best quality ingredients are sourced and their individual selection of herbs and spices used in the recipe creates their own unique flavour. With no artificial ingredients or preservatives, along with being low in fat and high in iron, all this makes it a very healthy product too.

Although the traditional black and white puddings remain extremely popular, Debbie and Richard are always keen to explore new products and opportunities for expansion. With exciting new products such as chilli black pudding and the fantastic gluten-free black pudding joining the classic recipes, this forward-thinking company is embracing the future while keeping the heritage of Bury's favourite product at its heart.

Now supplying over 12 countries around the world, The Bury Black Pudding Company are bringing this northern delicacy to the masses, whilst still maintaining all of its traditional values.

The Bury Black Pudding Company
LAMB HOTPOT WITH BLACK PUDDING

A Lancashire classic with the delicious addition of Bury Black Pudding.
Serves 4.

Ingredients

2 tbsp olive oil

1kg lamb neck, chopped

2 onions, sliced

½ tsp salt

1 tbsp plain flour

200ml lamb stock

1 sprig of fresh thyme

2 bay leaves

1 tbsp Worcestershire sauce

50g butter, cubed

2 x 200g Bury Black Pudding rings, sliced and skin removed

1kg potatoes, peeled and sliced

Salt and pepper

Method

Preheat the oven to 180°C.

Heat the oil in a pan and fry the lamb for a few minutes to brown. Remove from the pan and set aside. In the same pan, cook the onions for 2-3 minutes, then season with the salt. Stir in the flour. Add the stock a little at a time, then add the thyme, bay leaves and Worcestershire sauce. Stir and simmer for 8-10 minutes.

Grease a lidded casserole dish and place a layer of potatoes over the bottom of the dish. Season well. Spoon in half the browned lamb, then arrange half the black pudding slices on top. Pour over half the onion and stock liquid. Repeat the layering process until you have used up all the ingredients, making sure you finish with a top layer of potatoes.

Dot the top layer of potatoes with the butter, then cover with a lid and cook in the preheated oven for 20 minutes.

Remove the lid and cook for a further 20 minutes uncovered. Serve with your favourite vegetables.

The Daddy of
BLUE CHEESES

Best known for the phenomenally successful Blacksticks Blue, Butler's Farmhouse Cheeses boasts a proud pedigree of artisan cheese making from the family's own dairy cattle and goats.

Butler's Farmhouse Cheeses really is a family affair, from the family-owned farms that supply the milk, to the family business creating distinctive, delicious handmade cheeses at their dairy in Inglewhite at the foot of Beacon Fell.

Butler's traces its roots back to Richard and Annie Butler, who began making artisan farmhouse Lancashire cheese from their own dairy herd in 1932. The business was interrupted by the Second World War, then revived in 1956 by the couple's son Peter who lived at Blacksticks Farm. Today, Richard and Annie's granddaughter Gillian Hall and her husband Colin head the company, and their sons, Matthew and Daniel have recently joined the family firm too.

Over half of the milk used in the cheeses comes from the family's own farms – the dairy cows owned by Gill's brother Andrew at Wilson Fields and Lower Barker Farms, and the goats belonging to her niece Nicola at Throstle Nest Farm.

Butler's Peter Elvin said: "Nothing is made by machine. The biggest asset is our local milk produced with grass from the lush pastures around Beacon Fell.

"We make three different types of Lancashire cheese and other farmhouse varieties like Red Leicester. But what is unique about Butler's is as well as traditional English hard cheese, we make soft blue cheeses and soft Camembert-type white rinded cheese."

The company is renowned among cheese connoisseurs as the creator of Blacksticks Blue, launched in 2004.

Peter said: "It's softer and very much a milder, creamier cheese than a Stilton – it's more like a continental blue. The whacky thing we did was make it orange.

"We started selling it to local restaurants and at markets, then it was discovered by Marks and Spencer and has built up a following."

The popularity of Blacksticks Blue cheese, described by local celebrity chef Simon Rimmer as "the daddy of all blue cheeses," means the name will forever be associated with Butler's.

Butler's Farmhouse Cheeses
BLACKSTICKS BLUE BEEF STROGANOFF

A super-easy take on a classic recipe with the creamy taste and texture of Blacksticks Blue providing the perfect partner for the fillet steak. Serves 2, but can easily be scaled up.

Ingredients

200g fillet steak, cut into thin strips

1 small onion, finely sliced

1 clove garlic, crushed

Oil for frying

100ml hot chicken stock

125ml double cream

75g Blacksticks Blue cheese, crumbled into small pieces

Ground black pepper

Parsley, chopped, to garnish

Method

Heat the oil in a frying pan over a medium heat and soften the onion for about 5 minutes. Add the garlic and the steak. Brown the meat for a couple of minutes and add the stock. Allow to boil rapidly for a couple of minutes, stirring continuously to deglaze the pan.

Turn down the heat to low and stir in the Blacksticks Blue. Keep stirring until all the cheese has melted then turn off the heat. Swirl in the cream.

Season to taste and serve onto a warmed plate with rice or new potatoes and French beans.

A French influence in
LANCASHIRE

British food with a French feel dominates the menu at The Cartford Inn, where you'll also find delicious treats to take home from 'TOTI': their on-site delicatessen.

A 17th century coaching inn at the historic crossing of the River Wyre, boasting superb views of the Bowland Fells, The Cartford Inn specialises in modern British pub dining with personality. With the receipt of numerous regional and national awards (including recently being named Lancashire Tourism Pub of The Year) it's established itself as one Lancashire's best country inns, with a nationwide reputation for its outstanding food and drink as well as its friendly staff and unique style.

French-born owner Patrick Beaumé and his British wife Julie bring some continental flavours to the menu, which changes seasonally to reflect the best of local produce.

"The menu features updated British classics along with more adventurous cooking and of course there's a discernible French influence," says Patrick.

Benefitting from great relationships with local suppliers, the chefs make the most of outstanding local meat, poultry, cheeses, fruit and vegetables. Game from local shoots appears on the menu throughout the season alongside ingredients foraged from nearby fields and woodlands such as wild mushrooms.

Since taking over in 2007, the Beaumés have made significant developments to the site, including adding a riverside extension in 2011 incorporating a new dining room and increasing the inn's number of bedrooms to 15. In 2014 a new two-storey riverside facility for private and corporate events opened.

Julie said: "Since we bought the pub, we've constantly invested to improve experiences for visitors and impress our personalities on the location.

"Apart from being known for its food and its picturesque location, the inn is loved for its individuality and characterful, rural-chic décor and style."

The latest addition at the award-winning inn is TOTI (Taste of the Inn), an on-site deli opened in late 2015 that sells quality speciality produce, deli ingredients and their own freshly made products.

Patrick said: "There's lots of produce from the local area, such as Lancashire cheeses and handmade chocolates and Mediterranean store cupboard ingredients as you'd expect from a good deli, but there's a British focus and quality is most important."

"You can find everything to make a nice lunch without too much work. The idea is to create inspiration for people's cooking and encourage them to try new things."

The Cartford Inn

The Cartford Inn
PILLING MARSH LAMB BREAST WITH BLACK PEAS, SWEETBREADS, SHEEP'S CURD CHEESE, PEA PURÉE AND A WILD GARLIC AND MINT DRESSING

An adventurous dish by The Cartford Inn's head chef Chris Bury showcasing some outstanding produce including lamb from local farmer Ian Jenkinson, cheese and foraged wild garlic, plus black peas add a nod to Lancashire's food traditions.
Serves 4 as a starter.

Ingredients

For the lamb:

1 lamb breast, deboned

1 carrot

3 sticks celery

1 onion

1 bulb garlic

3 sprigs rosemary

2 litres lamb stock

For the black peas:

250g black peas

250ml vegetable stock

1 shallot, peeled and sliced

1 sprig thyme

Cider vinegar

For the pea purée:

250g freshly podded or frozen peas

1 shallot, diced

1 clove garlic, finely chopped

40g unsalted butter

For the wild garlic and mint dressing:

A small bunch of mint and a small bunch of wild garlic

Olive oil

12 sweetbreads from the throat

180g Leagram's sheep's curd cheese

Sea salt and freshly ground black pepper

Method

For the lamb and black peas:

Start 24 hours ahead by soaking the black peas in water, then eight hours ahead of when you want to eat, it's time to begin cooking the lamb.

Cut the lamb breast into three equally sized pieces. Roughly chop the carrot, celery and onion and split the garlic bulb in half. Place the lamb, chopped vegetables, garlic, rosemary and some seasoning into a deep, heavy casserole pan. Cover with the lamb stock and cook in preheated oven at 180°C for 3 hours.

When the lamb is cooked, remove from the pan and place the pieces on top of each other between two baking sheets. Press the lamb by placing weights on top and leaving to go cold before transferring to the fridge. When you come to serve the dish the proteins in the lamb will hold it together in one piece.

Drain the black peas and place in a pan with plenty of salted water. Bring to the boil and simmer for around an hour until the peas are just soft and their skins are coming off.

Drain the black peas and place in a pan with the vegetable stock, shallot, thyme and a teaspoon of cider vinegar. Heat and simmer until almost all the liquid has evaporated. Season with salt, pepper and a little vinegar to taste. Set aside.

For the pea purée:

Sweat the shallot and the garlic in the butter until soft. Add the peas to the pan, cover with water and bring to the boil. Cook the peas for 2-3 minutes and then drain off the water. Blitz the mixture in a blender and pass through a fine sieve to make it smooth.

For the dressing:

In a blender, blitz the mint and garlic leaves with enough olive oil to make a light consistency.

For the sweetbreads:

Blanch in boiling water and remove the outer membrane. Refresh in iced water.

Pan-fry in unsalted butter until the sweetbreads begin to colour. Slice the lamb breast into four pieces.

To serve:

Reheat the lamb in a hot oven for 5 minutes. Place a good amount of pea purée around each plate and set a lamb piece in the centre of each. Arrange the other cooked elements around the lamb, finishing with pieces of the sheep's curd cheese and the dressing.

Sausage HEAVEN

Local meat and home-mixed seasonings combine to mouth-watering effect in Cowman's Famous Sausages.

If sausages are your passion, you'll be in seventh heaven at Cowman's Famous Sausage Shop.

With more than 70 different types including a selection of gluten-free variations, plus seasonal variations and a sausage of the month, this unique butcher's shop in the heart of Clitheroe is an absolute treat for the sausage connoisseur.

Cowman's has been an established butchers on these premises for more than 120 years, and in addition to the extensive range of handmade sausages created from secret recipes handed down through three generations, they sell locally sourced cuts of beef, pork, lamb and poultry. Co-owners Paul Howard and Nick Gell both have a long standing relatonship with the butchers, between them working at Cowmans for a combined total of more than thirty years. They took over from Master Butcher Cliff Cowburn, whose family had run the business since the 1950s, and have been at the helm since May 2015.

Each Cowman's sausage contains at least 75 percent lean meat: and as their proclamation states 'no slurry, slurp or goo' and use pork from outdoor-reared pigs and beef and lamb from animals raised in the Bowland area. When combined with different herb and spice seasonings blended on the premises, it's no wonder they are award-winning butchers.

Cowman's oldest recipe is the old fashioned pork sausage, which was originally made by Cliff Cowburn's great-grandfather, while other family favourites, Cumberland and Lincolnshire sausages are made to traditional recipes with innovative flavours constantly being created and tested by their families and staff.

Paul said: "At Easter, we have chocolate chip and lime ones - they go down very well, and at Halloween our spiced pumpkin sausages are popular.

"When we produce a new one, it's a team effort. Someone comes up with an idea, ideally something unusual and innovative. We mix a seasoning to complement it, cook it up and see if we've got it right or whether it needs improving."

The master tasters at the shop test every new recipe, which include taste-bud tempting castle pork, made from wild boar, mead and black pudding; pork and caramelised onion; and Moroccan lamb.

So which is Paul's favourite?

"It depends what day it is, but we had the Linconshire at my wedding reception which went down a treat with all the guests," he says.

"I do like Highlander pork, which has the seasoning of a haggis but is made with pork; or pork and black pudding, or even venison..."

With such a huge variety to choose from, anyone would be hard-pressed to pick a favourite, and it seems Paul can't pick one either!

Cowman's Famous Sausages
CAJUN MELTING MOZZARELLA MEATBALLS

A real fusion of cuisines created by Paul's wife, Helena, with Cowman's Famous Sausage Shop sausages at its spicy and satisfying heart. Serves 2 large portions or 4 smaller.

Ingredients

For the meatballs:

8 Cowman's Famous Sausage Shop Cajun sausages (other flavours work well too)

3 spring onions, chopped

8 basil leaves, torn up

2 slices brown/multi seed bread (but any will work) blended into breadcrumbs

1 large egg

1 tsp paprika

1 good pinch of sea salt

1 pinch of pepper

1 tsp chilli flakes

20-30g grated Parmesan cheese to taste

15g plain flour

1 ball mozzarella cheese

For the sauce:

1 red onion, finely chopped

1 tbsp pesto

A good slosh of balsamic vinegar

Olive oil

2 tins chopped tomatoes

2 cloves garlic, finely chopped or 1 heaped tsp of garlic purée

Method

For the meatballs

Slice each sausage lengthways and peel off the skin. Place the meat into a large mixing bowl.

Add the chopped spring onions, egg, breadcrumbs, paprika, chilli flakes, Parmesan, flour, sea salt and pepper. Using your hands, mix everything together, then sprinkle in the basil leaves and gently fold into the mixture.

Chop the mozzarella roughly into 1-2cm cubed sized pieces. Take a small handful of the meatball mixture and roll into a ball about the size of a ping pong ball. Holding it in the palm of one hand, gently press your thumb into the ball to create a space to put the mozzarella into, then gently fold the mixture around the cheese. Make sure you can't see the cheese otherwise it will seep out whilst cooking.

For the sauce

Heat the olive oil in a deep frying pan, add the finely chopped red onion and garlic and cook for about 5 minutes. Add the balsamic vinegar, fry for a further 1-2 minutes, then add in the tinned tomatoes and pesto. Fry for a further 5 minutes.

To cook

Preheat the oven to 180°c.

Place all the meatballs into a ceramic roasting dish or casserole dish, layering them if necessary but ideally equally spaced. Pour over the sauce and cover the dish.

Cook in the oven for about an hour.

A Warm
WELCOME

A wow-factor building and a menu that mixes traditional afternoon teas with modern meals – plus a cocktail or two – is The Dearden Tea Rooms' recipe for success.

Steeped in history the original Victorian building was built in 1752 and remains a focal point of the town's architecture today. With many original features and antique furnishing throughout, The Dearden Tea Rooms is a delightful step back in time with some modern ingredients thrown into the mix. Opened in 2014 by Chris Hood and Andrea Britland, the tea rooms has a vintage feel from the original Lancashire range and open fire, to the fine china that the showstopper afternoon teas are served on.

Together Andrea, a former social worker, and Chris, a lifelong chef, have cooked up award-winning tea rooms worthy of regional recognition. The Dearden Tea Rooms is earning itself a real reputation for its luxurious afternoon teas, which are served with prosecco, Champagne, cocktails, or a choice of the vast selection of loose teas. Loose tea isn't their only speciality, there's a coffee for everyone too.

Chris is dedicated to sourcing local produce of the highest quality from reputable suppliers. The tea rooms offer a full menu from all-day breakfasts to sandwiches, burgers and light meals, to hearty dishes and homemade desserts. Andrea has followed her lifelong dream of running a tea room and spends every spare minute she has baking cakes and sweet treats for the many customers that visit the tea rooms in their droves each week.

They already believe they create the best afternoon tea in the area but they want to be known for the best afternoon tea in the North West. As a licensed premises, the tea room holds regular gin evenings and cheese and wine events. "We've been embraced by the local community and people coming from further afield," said Andrea. "The building has got the wow factor and that's important to the ambience we try to create when you come in."

Dearden Tea Rooms'
STICKY TOFFEE PUDDING

A luscious take on a proper sticky toffee pudding with homemade custard that'll have them queuing up for seconds. Serves 4-6.

Ingredients

For the sticky toffee pudding:

220g pitted dates

50g unsalted butter, softened, plus extra for greasing

150g dark brown sugar

2 tbsp golden syrup

2 tbsp black treacle

220g self-raising flour

2 free-range eggs

1½ tsp bicarbonate of soda

For the toffee sauce:

500ml double cream

175g unsalted butter

175g Demerara sugar

1 tbsp golden syrup

1 tbsp black treacle

For the custard:

200ml double cream

700ml whole milk

4 large egg yolks

3 tbsp cornflour

200g caster sugar

½ vanilla bean, split and scraped

Method

For the sticky toffee pudding

Grease a 1 litre/1¾ pint pudding basin with a little butter.

Put a heatproof plate in the bottom of a large saucepan. Fill the kettle and put it on to boil.

Place the dates in a pan with 200ml water. Cook for 3-4 minutes, then transfer to a food processor and blend. Set aside.

In a large bowl, beat the softened butter and dark brown sugar together until smooth.

Add the golden syrup, treacle, flour, eggs, bicarbonate of soda and the blended dates. Mix until combined.

Pour the mixture into the prepared basin. Fold a large piece of aluminium foil in half and grease one side with butter. Wrap the pudding in the greased foil, greased side facing into the pudding. (Pleat the foil a few times as you wrap it to allow room for the pudding to expand.) Secure the foil to the rim of the pudding basin with string.

Sit the basin on the plate inside the prepared saucepan. Place over a low heat and pour boiling water around the basin until it reaches half way up the side. Place a lid on the saucepan and steam the pudding for 2½-3 hours (check occasionally to make sure the water hasn't completely evaporated and top up with more boiling water if needed).

Remove the pudding from the pan, discard the foil lid and turn it out onto a plate.

For the toffee sauce

In a pan over a low heat, combine the cream, butter and sugar. When the butter and sugar have melted, whisk in the syrup and treacle.

For the custard

Put the cream and milk into a large pan and gently bring to just below boiling point.

Meanwhile, in a large bowl, whisk the egg yolks, cornflour, sugar and vanilla. Gradually pour the hot milk mixture onto the sugar mixture, whisking constantly.

Wipe out the saucepan and pour the mixture back into it. Heat gently, stirring with a wooden spoon until the custard thickens.

Quirky, creative and CONTEMPORARY

Take a trip to Preston's duk-pond and winedown or its Chorley Deli and Cantina for a Peruvian-themed experience and totally different style of service

When Andrea Mellon switched from a career in the travel industry to follow her foodie dreams in 2006, she retained her love of far-flung places in the menu.

duk-pond, her main restaurant in Preston, has a decidedly Peruvian influence that's echoed in the duk-pond deli and cantina in Chorley. Winedown, her third venue, is a cheese and wine cellar, based in the Preston building that was outgrown by the original duk-pond eatery.

Andrea's cuisine is eclectic, all-based on her own recipes, and the menu is packed with gluten-free, low salt, low fat and allergy-free alternatives. The approach when you come in for a meal is very different too.

Andrea said: "I'm a self-taught chef and only way I know to cook is with raw products straight into the pan, and I can generate anything for anyone at any time.

"I started to get a lot people saying 'can I have low fat or low salt?' or 'I'm allergic to strawberries' so we have a discussion.

"Staff have conversations with the guests about any allergies or intolerances, and we build up that rapport. We're a family company, we intend to stay that way, and we treat people like family - so they can have what they want."

The same culture is found throughout the three venues, where the food is vibrant, colourful and strong on presentation and attention to detail.

Although the duk-pond deli and cantina shares the Peruvian theme, the food that customers buy to take home or eat on the ground floor with a selection of unusual teas and coffees is sourced as locally as possible. Charcuterie and meat comes from nearby and a local lady makes gluten-free cakes and confectionary.

"The deli and cantina is very much a market to table mentality," says Andrea.

"It limits our carbon footprint because we go to the local fishmonger, butcher and vegetable sellers to conjure the menus from that day's purchase."

Winedown, she says, is like stepping into another world.

"There is an urban funky feeling of being underground and we have more than 150 wines and serve all local cheeses. Wine and cheese, what more do you need? Job done!"

duk-pond
PERUVIAN STEW

duk-pond's famous Peruvian Stew is a spicy vegan recipe with an unusual blend of fruit and vegetables, packed with flavours that shouldn't work together but do. Rich, delicious and decidedly good for you. Serves 4.

Ingredients

1 apple, pear, orange, mango, plum and fig (or fruit of your choice)

1 large tomato, courgette, butternut squash, yam and sweet potato (or vegetables of your choice)

1 small red onion, chopped

1 tin plum tomatoes

1 punnet each of strawberries, raspberries and blackberries

1 punnet mushrooms

100g flat leaf parsley

100g coriander

4 cloves garlic, chopped

6-8 red and green chillies, chopped

1 tsp Demerara sugar

Pinch of salt and pepper

Method

Cook together the suggested vegetables or your favourite alternatives in a heavy bottomed pan until they have softened but are still firm. There is no need to add water or oil. Set to one side.

Sauté the chillies, onion and garlic in a frying pan until soft. Add the sugar, salt and pepper, then set to one side.

Chop the fruit of your choice and sauté to soften, then combine in the heavy bottomed pan with the softened vegetables, onions, garlic and chillies.

Add the tinned tomatoes, mushrooms and berries. Mix in the roughly chopped fresh herbs, retaining some to sprinkle on as a garnish when you're ready to serve.

Cook the stew through until it's hot and serve with crusty bread.

duk-pond
MACHU PICCHU

A tasty take on steak, served with duk-pond's own goat's cheese butter and asparagus wrapped in Serrano ham. Serves 1, but easily scalable.

Ingredients

1 fillet steak, around 225g

Knob of duk-pond's homemade goat's cheese butter

Salt and pepper

3 spears asparagus

3 slices Serrano ham

20g flat leaf parsley, roughly chopped

Method

Blanch the asparagus in hot water for 2 minutes then plunge into iced water to stop the cooking process. Once cool, wrap each spear in a slice of Serrano ham.

Sear the steak in a hot oiled pan and season to taste. Cook until caramelised all around and set aside on a board.

Add the asparagus to the pan to crisp the Serrano ham on both sides.

Place the steak on a slate or board and top with the goat's cheese butter.

Put the Serrano covered asparagus spears on top and serve with a flurry of parsley.

A cup of something SPECIAL

Let the freshly-roasted scent draw you into the wonderful world of Exchange Coffee – and tea.

Walking into a coffee roasters where there are more than 35 different coffees – and over 65 teas – to choose from could be a tad intimidating, but that's not the case with Exchange Coffee.

"We're here to help," says general manager Richard Isherwood.

"Some people want to know the coffee varietals, how it was processed and tasting notes. Others come in and just want some really nice coffee for Sunday lunch."

Started in the mid-1980s by Mark Smith, Exchange Coffee has roasting shops in Clitheroe and Blackburn. The two Victorian coffee houses are full of antique furniture with William Morris wallpaper and oak panelling. Wandering past the sacks of raw coffee, you can sit and choose a brew of anything that is sold in the shop and have a bite to eat. Afterwards you can pick your chosen roast of coffee or loose leaf tea to take home.

Richard said: "It's all about the smell; you can be out shopping and the aroma of the coffee roasting daily will draw you in. The secret of great coffee is it's freshness."

There's also a wholesale roasting warehouse in an old Baptist chapel in Blackburn, supplying coffee to businesses across the North and online buyers nationwide. As well as a coffee bar on Blackburn market.

"We've added up that the seven key roasters here have more than 135 years' roasting experience between us. Depending on the person, we take almost a year to train someone to roast coffee. It's a science and an art."

Over the years, Exchange Coffee have earned more than 30 Great Taste awards. Many of the coffees come from ethically-sourced Rainforest Alliance growers while new micro-lot and Cup of Excellence coffees are represented too.

But it's not just about the coffee: speciality black, white, green, fruit teas and herbal tisanes along with coffee brewers, grinders and mugs complete the Exchange offering.

"It's the team's enthusiasm that shines through," said Richard.

"We continually taste amazing coffees and learn something new every day - and we want customers to share the adventure."

Exchange Coffee

Exchange Coffee
CLEVER DRIPPER BREW GUIDE

You may not be a trained barista or have expensive coffee shop equipment at home, but there's no reason why you can't enjoy a perfect cup of coffee the way the professionals make it.

Clever Dripper has created a great little brewer for home use that uses a French Press immersion brew method, which is then filtered through a paper to leave a clean finish. The unique feature is the shut off valve, which holds the water until pressed upward on top of a jug or mug.

This means brew times can be varied for different coffees, which other pour over methods are unable to do.

Our suggested times and quantities provide a starting point, but we always encourage experimenting for personal preferences. Have fun!

Equipment

Clever Dripper

Size 4 filter papers

Kettle

Weighing scales

22g freshly roasted coffee

350ml water just off the boil

Jug

Your favourite cup

Method

Place a size 4 filter paper in your Clever Dripper and flush through using freshly drawn boiled water to remove any paper taste. Discard the rinse water.

Grind 22g of freshly roasted coffee on a medium (cafetière) setting and add to the bottom the brewer.

Slowly add approximately 350ml of water just off the boil. After 45 seconds, gently break the crust of the bloom by stirring.

Add the lid and leave to stand for a further 2 minutes 15 seconds.

Place the Clever Dripper on top of a jug or mug to open the valve. The fresh coffee should draw down within 45 seconds.

Remove the brewer and place it on its coaster to catch any drips.

Enjoy your brew!

As nature INTENDED

Organic, sustainable, high-welfare and alternative food that 'hasn't been messed with' is the Gazegill Organics trademark.

Lower Gazegill Farm near Clitheroe has been in Emma Robinson's family for close to 500 years. Today, Emma and husband Ian O'Reilly operate the 250 acres which is home to dairy cattle, rare breed pigs and sheep – and so much more.

Visitors to the farm, which is open for tours and educational visits, can see unploughed flower meadows, medieval ridge and furrows, and the remains of the Roman road that once passed through the property, where Roman coins and leather pouches have been found.

The meadows are designated biological heritage sites and provide grazing for the Gazegill animals and a valued habitat for wildlife.

"The farm has been passed on through my family and I'm working my socks off to pass it to my family," says Emma, who is mum to two girls and boy.

"It's our job to keep it for future generations."

The seeds for what is now Gazegill Organics – a farm shop, organic dairy, educational charity and nationwide online food delivery service – were sown in 2007 when Ian and Emma decided to take the farm out of wholesale and concentrate on selling direct to customers.

Ian said: "We initially set a goal of 2015 to sell 100 percent of what we produced but we did it by 2014."

The farm shop sells the O'Reillys' own produce and carefully selected organic foods from the local area, plus a fantastic selection of organic deli products, herbs and edible flowers.

A real highlight is the raw milk from Emma's Dairy, produced by the Gazegill's dairy shorthorn herd. The dairy also processes organic milk from nearby farms, providing a year-round fair price for farmers.

Gazegill milks 60-65 of its own cows and Emma knows each one by name.

She said: "Dairy shorthorns are an old fashioned North West breed; they are small, red and white cows with good feet that are perfect for a dairy farm. Fifty years ago, every farm would have had these or Ayrshires.

"There a very few illnesses, and because of the herb meadows, they self medicate. Our oldest is 20; in intensive farming by the time cows are six, they've been milked to death."

The resulting milk is more of a golden yellow colour than white, similar to the milk everyone drank a few generations ago. Emma's Dairy sells pasteurised organic milk but is also blazing a trail with raw, untreated milk straight from its own herd, which can only legally be sold straight to the end user.

Ian said: "It appeals to people who understand the health benefits. It hasn't been heat treated, and it contains good bacteria and enzymes. It's an untampered food, like you would have found 50 or 60 years ago."

The dairy's pasteurised milk also differs from the norm because it has not been homogenised, so it retains the whole fat that settles as cream at the top. Gazegill produces whole, semi-skimmed and skimmed varieties that it sells to wholesalers, shops, schools and universities.

Everywhere you look at Lower Gazegill farm, there is livestock: from the dairy herd to sheep and pigs.

"It's a genuine open farm," says Emma.

"We've got pigs running around the yard; all that money people waste on gyms when they could come here and chase the pigs!"

Under Emma's parents, the backbone of the farm was dairy, but she and Ian have boosted the type of livestock on site. What the animals all have in common is that they're grass-fed, slow-grown and, says Emma, "reared with love."

There are a variety of pig breeds, each of which produces a darker meat than intensively-reared animals that is similar to wild boar.

Ian said: "The Oxford Sandy and Black pigs are like dogs; you tickle their bellies and they roll over. They are a good bacon pig. The Durocs are a meaty pig and the Berkshire crosses are good for sausages and salami. They all have different traits."

The farm has Welsh Mountain sheep, traditional Mule sheep and Hampshire Downs. Rose veal comes from the dairy shorthorns, and turkeys and geese are reared for Christmas. The Gazegill Organics farm shop also sells meat from beef shorthorns from a nearby farm, alongside local eggs and chicken. It's all sourced via the same type of fair trade model that governs Gazegill's dealings with fellow dairy farmers.

The butchery is a central part of the farm shop, which also sells products nationwide via online ordering. You'll find traditional cuts plus mutton and good stock bones, oils and lard that are harder to come by in the 21st century. As a proper butchery, it's also able to satisfy customer's demand for usual cuts and will even make up a sausage to your own recipe.

Gazegill Organics' vision of sustainable farming stretches further than the family holding and involves a mixture of education and initiatives that give something back to the community.

Lower Gazegill Farm has hosted school groups since the 1960s but in 2009, Ian and Emma opened a dedicated facility, which now handles around 250 visits a year from schools and other groups. The modern education centre at the farm provides training and activity days covering everything from healthy eating, horticulture and animal care to arts, crafts and social skills.

As well as the education project, the farm runs a Care Farm community interest company, where adults with mental health illnesses come to Lower Gazegill to grow herbs and edible flowers.

In the future, the farm aims to produce soup and other meals from ingredients grown at Lower Gazegill that can be gifted to local food banks, homeless shelters and elderly people. It already provides short-dated milk to a drop-in centre and food bank, and organic soup to a night shelter in Burnley.

This model of fairness runs through Gazegill Organics, from the way the O'Reillys treat their livestock, land and suppliers, to the wider community.

"We want to get the next generation of consumers behind sustainable agriculture, food and avoiding waste," said Ian.

"We want people to use real, untampered with food and to fall back in love with cooking."

Gazegill Organics
ROSE VEAL ESCALOPE

Make the most of organic ingredients in this classic rose veal dish, served with a zingy dressing. Serves 4.

Ingredients

For the rose veal:

4 organic rose veal escalopes, flattened (ask your butcher to flatten them with the side of a cleaver or you can do this at home with a wooden rolling pin)

Sea salt and black pepper to season

A little plain flour

1 medium organic egg

For the breadcrumbs:

3-4 slices fresh bread (crusty bread is great for this)

A shake of cayenne pepper

A good shake of smoked paprika powder

A shake of chilli powder

A good grind of sea salt and black pepper

For the dressing:

6 organic spring onions

A handful of fresh organic peas in their pods

A handful of fresh coriander and parsley, finely chopped

Cold pressed extra virgin olive oil

Raw clear honey (or good equivalent)

1 lemon, juiced with a little of the zest grated

1 tsp English mustard

Method

For the dressing

Add a good glug or two of olive oil (about 2-3 tablespoons) and then combine with 1-2 tablespoons of raw honey, 1 teaspoon of mustard, lemon juice and a little zest in a bowl. Pod the peas into the dressing and finely slice the spring onions into the mixture. Add the coriander and parsley and mix well so everything is coated.

For the veal and breadcrumbs

Cube the bread and blitz in a blender. Mix together in a bowl with the spices and seasonings.

If your veal needs thinning, do it now with a wooden rolling pin on a heavy wooden chopping board. You want the escalopes to be about 8mm thick so they cook quickly.

Beat the egg. Coat the veal with the flour and then dip into the egg until covered and coat generously with the breadcrumb mixture. Set aside and chill for 15 minutes.

In a heavy pan, heat olive oil on a moderate heat and fry the veal until golden brown, turning once. Remove from the heat and rest for a minute or two.

To serve

Spoon a generous amount of the dressing over the veal, making sure the peas and spring onions are shared well.

This dish tastes great with sautéed white or sweet potatoes.

Simple ELEGANCE

Magnificent views of award-winning gardens accompany the relaxed dining experience at Gibbon Bridge Hotel, where local Lancashire produce dominates the menu.

Back in 1982, Janet Simpson and her late mother Maggie, diversified from the family farm and their cake and pie stall at Blackburn market to open a restaurant with rooms. From those seeds came Gibbon Bridge Hotel that today boasts 30 bedrooms, 23 acres of award-winning gardens and a destination restaurant that attracts regulars from across the North West.

Baking remains an integral part of the mix. The hotel has its own bakery producing bread and desserts, including scrumptious apple pies, both for the restaurant and for diners to take out. Delicious preserves can also be ordered to take a taste of Gibbon Bridge home with you.

Fresh fruit, vegetables and herbs are grown in the kitchen gardens. Poultry is sourced from Johnson and Swarbrick, near Preston, for Gibbon Bridge's slow-cooked crispy duckling. Leagram organic dairy provides the Lancashire cheeses for the light and fluffy soufflés, and Ann Forshaw – an old friend of Janet's who now sells to Sainsbury's – supplies yoghurt.

Janet said: "We're a network of people who all started off together and we all know each other."

Longevity of relationships is important at Gibbon Bridge, with many of the people working at the hotel having been with the business since the early days. But the hotel and restaurant have also adapted with the times, to ensure diners have a comfortable as well as delicious experience.

Janet said: "The restaurant is very light and airy and overlooks our beautiful gardens. It's friendly with a nice relaxed feel. We have linen table cloths and an atmosphere of simple elegance. Ideal for a special occasion. For more casual dining our alfresco areas offer a unique alternative.

"We have lots of regulars during the week who travel from Manchester, Cheshire and Yorkshire for lunch, as well as locals and tourists."

The three-course Sunday lunch, which like everything in the restaurant is prepared fresh to order, is hugely popular.

"We're all about great food and great service, and we continue to move with the times. But we also know the importance of the tried and tested approach that our customers love."

Gibbon Bridge Hotel

Gibbon Bridge Hotel

LOIN OF LAMB TOPPED WITH A SPINACH & MINT MOUSSE & A PUFF PASTRY LATTICE

The fresh spring flavours of lamb, mint and spinach,
served with a ruby red jus. Serves 4.

Ingredients

For the mousse:

1 chicken breast

Salt and pepper

1 egg

284ml double cream

150g spinach, chopped

Handful of mint leaves

For the lamb:

1 full loin of lamb

Pig caul fat (available from your butcher)

300g puff pastry

1 egg

For the jus:

500ml good homemade beef stock

284ml Port or red wine

2 tbsp redcurrant jelly

½ tsp chopped thyme

Method

For the mousse

First make the mousse by blitzing the chicken in a blender. Wait for it to form a ball, then add a pinch of salt, the spinach and mint, and blitz again. Add one egg and the double cream and blend again. Be careful not to over-blend as it will split the cream. Refrigerate until required.

For the lamb

Next remove any fat or sinew from the loin of lamb. Spread the mousse on one side of the lamb so it matches the size of the eye of the meat.

Wrap it in the pig caul fat and then in cling film. Tie each end so it makes a flat cylinder. Place in a water bath and cook for 1 hour at 64°C.

Meanwhile, roll out the puff pastry and egg wash it with the remaining egg. Cut with a lattice cutter.

After an hour, remove the meat from the water bath and remove the cling film. Wrap the pastry around the meat and mousse and cook immediately in the oven at 225°C for 5-7 minutes or until the pastry is a golden brown.

If you are not using a water bath do not wrap in cling film instead place the lamb topped with the mousse and wrapped in the pig caul fat in the oven at 225°C for 5 minutes. Remove and wrap the pastry around the meat and mousse and cook immediately in the oven at 225°C for 5-7 minutes or until the pastry is a golden brown.

For the jus

Reduce the Port or red wine by a third and add the beef stock, redcurrant jelly and thyme. Simmer until the sauce coats the back of a spoon.

To serve

Cut the loin into 4 pieces and pour the sauce around. Serve with your choice of vegetables.

A trio of TASTES

Three different venues with three different flavours taking your on a culinary trip from New York to the Mediterranean.

Lytham on the Fylde coast boasts three top eating and drinking destinations run by the same team – Henry's Bar and Grill, Capri and Barrique.

Henry's, which opened in 2009, takes its inspiration from a New York steakhouse, and is also known for its superb fish dishes. Head chef Matthew Hardacre was born and bred locally and is a big fan of local produce. He's using his unique style to bring out the best in fresh, seasonal Lancashire ingredients.

He said: "You just need to look outside to be inspired, seeing the coast, and creating dishes with fresh fish from Lanigans... what could be better?"

Capri, based in a Grade II listed building, opened in 2012 and enjoys a chic European ambience, with a sun-drenched terrace and beautiful interior. Serving food from breakfast time through to evening meals, everything is made fresh in-house including the pastas, pizza bases and ice creams. It's a place to enjoy a celebration lunch with the family or raise a glass to an evening out with friends.

Barrique, the newest of the trio, is also part of a Grade II listed building, Lytham's Market Hall. Barrique – named after an oak wine barrel – is a wine shop, bar and deli, located in the heart of town.

It serves wines from around the world, which are available to drink inside or take home, or you can enjoy a bite to eat while relaxing with a coffee. There's a great choice of meats and cheeses sourced from Lancashire suppliers, which again are available to buy at the deli or eat in at Barrique.

Barrique director, Jake Crimmin, a former sommelier at Jamie Oliver's Fifteen restaurant and head sommelier at Gaucho, said: "The deli side has a mix of Spanish food and local cheeses and deli products.

"There is a lack of wine shops that have a food offering as well. We do small tapas and our strapline is that we're a place where people can enjoy wine and explore taste."

Henry's Bar & Grill, Capri and Barrique

Henry's Bar and Grill
LAMB HASH WITH LAMB CHOPS

Herby and garlicky lamb hash combined with lamb chops, vibrant veggies and a rich red wine sauce makes this an impressive dinner party winner. Serves 4-6

Ingredients

For the lamb hash and lamb chops:

1 lamb shoulder

12 lamb chops

200ml red wine

Rosemary and thyme sprigs

1 bulb garlic (keep 2 cloves for the potato mix)

200ml chicken stock

5 potatoes, half-cooked and grated

2 carrots, grated

2 shallots, finely diced

2 tbsp dried mint

For the red wine sauce:

500ml good quality beef stock

500ml red wine

2 cloves garlic

2 shallots, finely sliced

1 sprig thyme

100g butter, diced

For the vegetables:

1kg carrots, peeled and chopped

2 shallots, finely sliced

2 cloves garlic

½ a block of butter plus 2 knobs for the spinach

2 bags of baby spinach, washed

Method

For the lamb hash and lamb chops

Brown the lamb shoulder all over. In the meantime, sweat the garlic, rosemary and thyme sprigs for a minute then add the wine and bring to the boil.

Add the chicken stock, then pour over the browned lamb. Cover with parchment then tin foil and braise in the oven at 150°C for 2 hours.

When cool, remove the fat and flake the meat. Add the grated potatoes, carrots, shallots and dried mint and mix thoroughly.

Mould into 70ml cutter and fry in a hot pan, flipping over when browned. Put into the oven for 10 minutes.

Sear the lamb chops in a smoking hot pan until browned all over and the fat is golden. Rest for a few minutes.

For the red wine sauce

Sweat the garlic and shallots until soft, then add the red wine and reduce by two-thirds. Add the beef stock and reduce again by half. Take off the heat and add the butter bit by bit until the sauce has a nice shine.

For the vegetables

Put the carrots, shallots and garlic in a pan, cover with water and boil until soft.

Strain, then mix in the half block of butter and blitz to purée. Check the seasoning.

Melt the additional two knobs of butter in a pan, add the spinach and wilt until just cooked.

To serve

Swipe the carrot purée on the plate, place the buttered spinach in a little mound with the lamb hash on top, lay the lamb chops on the hash and drizzle with the red wine sauce.

Barrique Bar
HAM CROQUETAS

A tasty and very moreish Spanish-style tapas recipe that is surprisingly simple to make. Makes about 30.

Ingredients

For the béchamel sauce:

500ml whole milk

1 onion, halved

1 bay leaf

2 clove

50g butter

50g plain flour

For the croquetas:

250g good quality Serrano ham in one piece

4 dsp olive oil

120g unsalted butter

115g plain flour

1 litre full fat milk

½ tsp nutmeg

1 tbsp Parmesan cheese, grated

3 eggs, beaten

250g breadcrumbs

Method

In a small saucepan gently boil the milk. Add the onion, studded with the bay and cloves Turn off the heat and leave to infuse for 20 minutes.

In another saucepan melt the butter, then add the flour.

Stir continuously it forms a roux. Continue cooking for another 2 minutes.

Remove the onion, bay and cloves from the milk. Add the milk to the roux gradually, stirring as you go, until you get a smooth sauce.

Cook on a low heat for 5-10 minutes stirring occasionally then season to taste.

Cut the ham into 0.5cm cubes. Heat the oil and butter in a heavy bottomed pan and gently fry the ham until most of the fat is rendered off (about 8 minutes).

Stir in the flour and continue to cook over a low heat for a further 10 minutes, stirring almost constantly.

Put the milk into another pan and gently warm until the milk is just below a simmer. Take the pan with the ham off the heat. Gradually beat the milk with a hand whisk into the ham and flour mixture.

Return the pan back to a low heat, stirring all of the time until you reach a smooth béchamel sauce.

Add the nutmeg and Parmesan and cook for a further 8 minutes.

Remove the pan from the heat and transfer the béchamel to a large bowl. Allow to cool slightly. Cover the surface with cling film pressing it down onto the béchamel to prevent a skin from forming.

Put it into the fridge for a minimum of 4 hours.

To make the croquetas, arrange the beaten egg and breadcrumbs into two separate bowls. Carefully scoop a dessertspoon of béchamel and form into a croquette shape. Dip first into egg and then roll in breadcrumbs. Repeat with the remainder of the mixture.

Either heat a frying pan of oil to 180°C and fry the croquetas in batches for 2-3 minutes, or grill on a high heat, turning frequently until golden brown.

Serve while hot.

Capri
CHORIZO AND 'NDUJA RISOTTO

A sunshine taste of Italy courtesy of this meaty and full-flavoured risotto in a rich, creamy sauce. Serves 4-6.

Ingredients

300g Arborio rice

1 shallot, finely diced

1 clove garlic, finely chopped

1 sprig thyme

175ml white wine

750ml chicken stock

300g chorizo, diced

2 tbsp 'nduja paste

2 red peppers, roasted, skinned and sliced

2 tbsp Parmesan cheese, grated

1 tbsp mascarpone cheese

Fresh basil

Method

Sweat the garlic, shallot and thyme until translucent. Add the rice and cook for a few minutes, stirring at short intervals. Add the wine and boil until it has all been absorbed by the rice, stirring constantly.

Add the stock a little at a time, again stirring constantly, allowing the rice to absorb the stock before adding any more.

In the meantime, fry the chorizo until crispy, then add it, the 'nduja paste and red peppers to the risotto rice.

Stir in the Parmesan and mascarpone, check the seasoning, and scatter over the fresh basil leaves to serve.

From farm shop to RESTAURANT

Local ingredients, an on-site bakery and a meat counter headed by an internationally renowned butcher makes Huntley's Country Stores a fantastic foodie day out.

There's a butcher, a baker and if not a candlestick maker, there is a furniture and antique shop where you might find some, along with a restaurant and ice cream parlour at Huntley's Country Stores.

Originally a farm shop, Huntley's started to sell local milk, meat and homemade ice cream after the 2001 foot and mouth outbreak. It has now been developed into an award-winning outlet village that has been owned by farmers, Harry and Lynn Wilson, since 2012.

At the heart of Huntley's is local, homemade produce that's for sale in the farm shop and served up in the restaurant. The artisan bakery is a seven-day-a-week operation, turning out traditional bread, cakes, pies and pastries for the shop and restaurant. You'll also find a fabulous fishmonger, a superb selection of seasonal vegetables, homemade preserves and wine and beer.

Huntley's ethos is quality and the meat sold from the butchery counter is one of the key attractions for customers.

Self-confessed "massive foodie" and head of butchery Tom Wood hails from farming stock that shows its pedigree Pope Simmental cattle around the UK and sells its bulls at the famous Stirling auctions. He's also a member of the Great Britain butchery team that showcases its skills competing internationally and demonstrating the craft at auctions and agricultural sales.

"I was brought up in it since I was a young lad," he says.

"I'm from a farming family and I can go out and select what I want, so I know it's up to my standards. The meat's all locally sourced from the Ribble Valley, I buy it all in on the bone and we can diversify any way the customer wants it.

"Butchery is becoming fashionable again. If anyone comes in and they want something, we go out of our way to give them it. We're not hidden away in a room and people see us preparing the meat behind the counter.

"I love the banter with the customers and the satisfaction they get from getting the produce they want."

Huntley's Country Stores
BEEF SHORT RIBS

Delicious tender slow-cooked ribs in a rich red wine sauce that's a fabulous dish for entertaining or a relaxed weekend supper. Serves 4.

Ingredients

Olive oil, for frying

6 thick-cut meaty beef short ribs

1 large garlic bulb, cut in half horizontally

1 heaped tbsp tomato purée

750ml red wine

1 litre beef stock

150g smoked bacon lardons

200g frozen silverskin onions

150g garden peas

3-4 carrots, peeled and sliced

250g small chestnut mushrooms, trimmed and halved

Sea salt and freshly ground black pepper

Flat leaf parsley, chopped, to garnish

Method

Preheat the oven to 170°C.

Heat a deep-sided roasting tray on the hob and add a glug of olive oil. Season the short ribs thoroughly, then fry for 10–15 minutes to brown really well on all sides. Add the silverskin onions to the tray and fry off to get some colour on them.

Add the halved and unpeeled garlic head, cut side down, pushing it to the bottom of the pan. Add the tomato purée and heat for a minute or two to cook it out. Pour in the wine to deglaze the pan, scraping up the bits at the bottom.

Bring to the boil and cook for 10-15 minutes until the liquid has reduced by half, then add stock to nearly cover the ribs (you'll need less stock if your roasting tray isn't very large). Bring to the boil again, basting the ribs with the juices.

Add the carrots, then cover the roasting tray with foil and cook in the preheated oven for 3-4 hours, basting now and then until the meat is tender and falling away from the bone.

About 10 minutes before the short ribs are ready to come out, fry the bacon lardons for 2-3 minutes until crisp and golden. Add the mushrooms and cook for 4-5 minutes until tender. Drain off any excess fat.

When the short ribs are ready, remove them from the oven and transfer to a serving dish. Squeeze the garlic cloves out of their skins and pass through a sieve. Spoon off any excess fat from the beef cooking liquid, then strain it through the sieve and mix with the garlic. If the sauce is too thin, reduce it by heating for a further 10-15 minutes after straining.

Add the peas to the cooking liquor at the last minute just to warm them through.

Serve the short ribs topped with the hot bacon lardons and mushrooms, with the sauce poured around. Garnish with chopped flat leaf parsley.

Huntley's Country Stores

T. Wood

Moroccan Lamb Sausage
Spicy and Hot
£8.10kg

Huntley's Country Stores
WILD MUSHROOMS ON TOAST WITH A CREAMY MUSTARD SAUCE

A flavour-packed lunch dish that makes the most of in-season foraged (or shop bought) wild mushrooms. Serves 4-6.

Ingredients

400g mixed wild mushrooms

200g smoked pancetta

500ml double cream

50ml white wine

2 tbsp white wine vinegar

1 tbsp wholegrain mustard

50g butter

Olive oil for frying

Brioche buns or loaf to serve

Dressed mixed salad leaves, to garnish

Flat leaf parsley, to garnish

Salt and pepper to season

Method

For the sauce

In a hot saucepan, reduce the vinegar and white wine to a syrup, then add the cream and butter. Reduce for a further 5 minutes until thickened, add the mustard and season with salt and pepper.

For the mushrooms

Cook the pancetta in olive oil in a hot frying pan until golden brown. Remove and set aside.

In the same pan, add a splash of olive oil and sauté the mushrooms, ensuring there is enough room in the pan for even cooking. If the pan is too small, fry off in batches. Add a knob of butter to finish the mushrooms, then season with salt and pepper.

Add the pancetta back to the pan with enough sauce to cover the mushrooms and reduce for a further 2-3 minutes.

To serve

While the sauce is reducing, toast the brioche.

Add chopped flat leaf parsley to the mushrooms and spoon onto the toasted brioche. Serve with the dressed mixed salad leaves.

Chill out in the
COUNTRYSIDE

A chilled out atmosphere and a menu featuring plenty of local game, meat and fish means The Inn at Whitewell is the perfect spot to kick back and relax after a day exploring the Lancashire countryside.

Dating back to the 1300s and retaining plenty of original features, The Inn at Whitewell is a proper old-fashioned stopping-off point where you can kick off your wellies after a walk with the dog and tuck into some top Lancashire nosh.

The Inn has been owned by the Bowman family for three generations. Current custodian Charles is the son of former Lancashire cricketer and brewer Richard, who was behind much of the restoration of the building that sits on the banks of the River Hodder and looks out across the Forest of Bowland.

Local brews are big behind the bar and locally-sourced food makes up much of the menu, where you'll find in-season game such as grouse from Lancashire Moor and partridge from Dunsop, venison dishes, plus beef and lamb from Burholme Farm. Fish is locally sourced from the Lancashire coast and there is a great selection of wines, too, with more than 20 available by the glass.

Head chef, Jamie Cadman, said: "My sous chefs, Gemma and James have been an integral part of the Whitewell's kitchen team now for a good number of years, and without their talent, dedication and determination to consistently produce such a high standard of food, we wouldn't be where we are today."

The Inn's ethos is a relaxed and friendly service, which attracts locals for the food and people from all over the UK for the chance to get away from it all and experience the spectacular scenery.

Diners can eat in the bar, where dogs are welcome too, at lunch time or in the evening, plus the dining room is open for evening meals. The ambience, which majors on relaxation, mixes up contemporary décor with the Bowman family's collection of antiques.

"People feel happy in their wellingtons with their dogs, and after a windswept walk you can come in and not have to dress up."

The Inn at Whitewell
PAN-FRIED KING SCALLOPS

Served with cauliflower purée, roasted cauliflower and pomegranate salad and hazelnut dressing. Serves 4.

Ingredients

12 king scallops (3 per person)

For the salad:

1 small head of cauliflower (half for the purée and half for roasting)

Seeds from ½ a pomegranate

1 bunch flat leaf parsley, roughly chopped

20g salted butter

2 tbsp groundnut oil

Salt and pepper

For the dressing:

3 tbsp groundnut oil

½ tbsp balsamic vinegar

½ tbsp lemon juice

40g hazelnuts, roasted and chopped

1 tsp French mustard

1 tsp maple syrup

Method

Make the dressing by whisking all the ingredients together in a bowl, then set aside.

Chop half the cauliflower into small pieces, put into a pan with the butter, salt and pepper and cover with water. Cook until tender.

Meanwhile, split the other half of the cauliflower into small equal sized florets, place in bowl with a little groundnut oil, salt and pepper, mix well and roast in the oven for about 15 minutes at 200°C until golden brown.

When the boiled cauliflower is tender, drain and purée in a food processer or pass through a fine sieve and keep warm.

Sear the scallops in a hot pan with a little oil for approximately 2-3 minutes on each side.

To serve

Mix the roast cauliflower, pomegranate seeds and parsley in a bowl with the dressing, and arrange on warmed plates with the cauliflower purée and king scallops.

The Inn at Whitewell
CONFIT SHOULDER OF LAMB AND JERSEY ROYAL TERRINE

A succulent dish combining tender lamb, new potatoes, spring vegetables and lamb jus favoured with redcurrant jelly and balsamic vinegar. This is a real favourite at The Inn. Serves 4.

Ingredients

For the lamb:

800g lamb shoulder, boned

500ml duck fat

1 bulb garlic

50g coarse sea salt

3 sprigs thyme leaves

For the Jersey Royal terrine:

500g Jersey Royal potatoes

75g clarified butter plus olive oil

For the spring vegetables:

½ celeriac

12 asparagus spears

120g peas

200g spinach

handful of pea shoots

3 onions

Olive oil

200ml milk

Butter

1 sprig fresh mint

Salt and pepper

For the lamb jus:

400ml browned chicken stock

400ml white wine

1 tbsp redcurrant jelly

2 tbsp balsamic vinegar

Knob of butter

Method

Ideally the shoulder and terrine should be made a day in advance so they're cool enough to slice.

For the lamb

Using a pestle and mortar, combine the peeled garlic, salt and thyme to make a rub which is then applied to both sides of the shoulder.

Lay out a piece of tin foil with baking parchment on top, place the lamb shoulder on it and roll up. Put into a baking tray, add the duck fat and slowly cook in the oven at 120°C for 4 hours until tender.

Unwrap the shoulder to cool slightly, then using the same method as above, re-roll the shoulder making sure it is tight and in a cylinder shape. Refrigerate until set.

For the Jersey Royal terrine

Lightly wash the potatoes to remove any dirt and slice as thinly as possible. Dress the potatoes with a little olive oil. In a parchment-lined terrine, layer the potatoes, seasoning with salt and pepper and add a little butter through every layer.

Cover with tin foil and bake at 170°C for about 1 hour. When cooked, it's important to press the terrine, then leave to cool and set in the fridge.

For the spring vegetables

Peel the celeriac and slice into a pan with the milk and a knob of butter, then simmer until tender. Blend the celeriac by adding a little of the milk it was cooked in, plus salt and white pepper to taste.

Slowly cook the onions with a knob of butter, salt and pepper, until caramelised.

Peel the asparagus from about halfway down the spear and then remove the tips and slice the rest to a similar size. Blanch in salted boiling water with the peas, spinach and pea shoots. Dress with olive oil and fresh mint.

For the lamb jus

In a saucepan, reduce the wine and balsamic vinegar down almost to a syrup, then add the stock and further reduce by two-thirds, whisking in the jelly and butter at the end to finish.

To finish the dish

Slice the shoulder into four pieces and gently fry until golden. While the lamb is cooking, remove the potato terrine from its mould and slice into 4 equal cross sections, then place into the oven for 10 minutes to warm.

Serve with the warm celeriac, caramelised onions, spring vegetables and jus.

John 'Gilly' Gillmore's
PROPER LANCASHIRE 'HOT' POT

Born in 'old' Lancashire, John Gillmore or Gilly to his BBC Radio Lancashire listeners, is a true champion of what's best about the county. His weekday four-hour lifestyle programme, highlighting the best of Lancashire's events, things to do, places to see and of course some of its fantastic food, has helped earn him a county tourism superstar award. And he's keen to showcase the superstar food that's on offer in Lancashire too. This is a spicy twist on one of the Red Rose county's signature dishes, for those with adventurous tastes. Serves 4-6.

Ingredients

For the seasoned flour:

50g plain flour

1 tsp sea salt

1 tsp freshly ground black pepper

1 tbsp dried thyme / 2 tbsp fresh chopped thyme (dried herbs are stronger than fresh, they're more concentrated)

For the hotpot:

6 best neck end or shoulder lamb chops – about 700g in total

1.2kg floury potatoes such as King Edwards, peeled and sliced fairly thinly

2 onions, chopped

3 carrots, sliced

2 tbsp garlic, minced (from a jar is fine)

1 tbsp red chillies, minced (from a jar is fine)*

2 tbsp chilli oil

1 litre lamb or beef stock (homemade if possible – otherwise a good quality shop bought one)

2 tbsp olive oil and knob of butter for frying

250ml merlot

Knob of butter

*If you don't like hot stuff, leave out the chillies and replace the chilli oil with 50g butter

Method

Grease a large casserole dish and preheat the oven to 160°C.

Mix the flour, sea salt, black pepper and thyme to make a seasoned flour. Toss the chops in it, ensuring they are evenly coated.

Heat two tablespoons of olive oil in a large heavy bottomed frying pan, and once hot, brown the chops for a few minutes on each side. You may want to do this in two batches. Cover the chops with foil and place to one side.

Add a knob of butter to the frying pan and when hot, add the onions and carrots and cook for about 5 minutes, stirring well, until they begin to soften. Add the garlic and one tablespoon of minced chillies. Stir well then pour the mixture into a bowl.

De-glaze the frying pan by pouring 250ml merlot into the hot pan, stirring with a wooden spoon to loosen all the bits from the pan. Then melt in the knob of butter.

Line the bottom of the casserole dish with a thin layer of sliced potatoes, season with salt and pepper, then add two chops and a third of the onion and carrot mix. Repeat until all the chops and carrot/onion is used up, then pour the merlot juice over the hotpot.

You should have enough potatoes left for a double layer on top of the dish. Place one layer, then pour over some meat stock until it is almost level with the top of the potatoes - it shouldn't quite come to the top, there should be a little gap. Brush the top of the potatoes with 1 tbsp chilli oil (or melted butter) and season.

Put the last layer of potatoes over the top of the dish, then brush the top of the potatoes all over with 1 tbsp chilli oil (or melted butter) and season.

Put the casserole in the oven at 160°C for 90 minutes to 2 hours. Test it's cooked by poking a skewer through the layers to check they are soft, then turn up to 200°C for up to 30 minutes to crisp the top. When it's done, the top layer should be well browned and crispy.

Serve with red cabbage or pickles, or a chunk of good crusty bread to mop up the juices.

Power in NUMBERS

Made In Lancashire's networking approach supports the county's food businesses and consumers with a think, buy and eat local ethos.

Born out of the 2001 foot and mouth crisis as a vehicle to help farmers diversify, Made In Lancashire is now a network boasting around 70 members ranging from artisan food producers to hospitality and retail businesses.

The network is based at Myerscough College and exists to big up Lancashire food and drink, with support to promote products and businesses, whether that's advice for new starters or helping established companies to find new markets.

That's all aided and abetted by the increasing interest and appreciation from people in the county about where their food comes from, according to Made In Lancashire's Rachel Oliver.

She said: "It's coming back into fashion - everybody wants to know exactly where their products are coming from and that they are fully traceable.

"They're supporting local businesses, because the quality is better, especially in organic fruit and vegetables. Lots of consumers are willing to pay more if it means knowing where their food and drink comes from."

Made In Lancashire is an active network that also puts members in touch with each other. The annual Meet the Local Producer event links up small, artisan makers and promotes them to the public and potential buyers from across the hospitality and retail sector - showing off what they do best.

There are three categories of members: retail, hospitality and producer, with membership costs depending on the size of the business. Members range from one man or woman bands making goodies in the kitchen at home to large and expanding businesses.

Being a part of Made in Lancashire means businesses benefit from the combined power of the group to share what they are doing on social media, to publicise events they are attending and find out about upcoming opportunities such as trade shows, farmers' markets and local food festivals. The network even hires out gazebos and equipment for newbies attending fairs and exhibitions, and hands out members' leaflets and business cards at events it attends.

Whether you're a food business or a food lover, Made In Lancashire is a great starting point for your think, buy and eat local journey through the county's finest produce.

Made in Lancashire
GOATHERD'S PIE

A change from the usual shepherd's pie, using minced goat from Cockerham Boer goat meat at Cockerham, near Lancaster. Serves 4-6.

Ingredients

500g Cockerham Boer goat mince

1 medium onion, chopped

2 carrots, sliced

1 mug of peas

A splash of Worcestershire sauce

1 lamb or vegetable stock cube

Fresh rosemary, finely chopped

Fresh mint, finely chopped

1 clove garlic, crushed or equivalent garlic purée

1 chilli (optional)

3 large potatoes

45ml milk

Knob of butter

Handful of grated mild cheese

Method

Brown the onion in a large pan, then add the goat mince and brown through.

Put the potatoes on to boil and cook for 15-20 minutes. Leave the skins on if you want a more rustic mash.

Once the mince is browned, pour it into a sieve to drain off any fat before placing back in the pan.

Add the herbs, Worcestershire sauce, crumbled stock cube, garlic, chilli (if using), peas and carrots. Cook for a further 5-10 minutes until the vegetables start to soften.

Preheat the oven to 190°C.

Drain the potatoes and mash with the milk and butter. Place the mince and vegetable mixture in an ovenproof dish and cover with the mash. Sprinkle over the cheese.

Place in the oven to bake for 25-30 minutes.

The Ice Cream LADY

Ice cream made using milk from the family's own dairy farm and a focus on honest Lancashire ingredients, making Mrs Dowson a real local food hero.

"Yes, Mrs Dowson is really a person," says Amanda Dowson. "She's me."

The ice cream brand that bears her name is truly a family affair. Husband Eric and son Ethan make the many-flavoured treat, son Elliot works on the family's Hawkshaw dairy farm that supplies the milk, and daughter Amelia works at the farm visitor centre, which opened in 2008.

The brand's rainbow logo was designed by the children and Amanda says she's "still looking for the pot of gold at the end."

Mrs Dowson's, like many Lancashire farm diversifications, started after the foot and mouth crisis. With a sweet-toothed family with a passion for ice cream and plenty of milk at their disposal, it was the obvious way to go.

Amanda said: "Family is at the heart of everything we do, and ice cream is no exception. Being total ice cream lovers we decided to invest in a small ice cream maker and make our own ice cream using only natural, honest ingredients. And so the story began.

"On the farm the whole family has an input when it comes to creating and developing new flavours of ice cream. Ultimately the taste test has always been the young Dowson children who have the final say on flavours.

"We utilise milk from our own herd of dairy cows, as well as championing local Lancashire producers wherever possible. This results in wonderful award-winning ice creams."

Having farmed the fields in the heart of the Ribble Valley for three generations, the Dowson's family farm has transformed from humble beginnings and now offers an exciting family visitor experience not to be missed.

Down on the farm, they are passionate about giving children and families the opportunity to get up close and join the team during the most exciting times of the farming calendar. With events including Lambing Live, Nature Trails and MooCow Safari, there is something to keep the whole family entertained.

Over the years the Dowson farm has grown and become home to over 250 dairy cows, farming over 300 acres of rolling hills and pasture land producing milk and cream which is used to create the finest ice cream in the area.

"As a lovely lady at the WI said: 'a kiss without a squeeze is like apple pie without the cheese.'"

Mrs Dowsons Ice Cream

Mrs Dowson's Ice Cream

THE PERFECT PANCAKES AND ICE CREAM

The Dowson family's favourite way to enjoy the ice cream that bears mum Amanda's name. Amanda says: "Whilst discussing this recipe over lunch and which flavour of ice cream to use, this was our conclusion: Elliott and Ethan – chunky chocolate; Amelia - Amaretto and black cherry; hubby Eric had treacle toffee with chocolate coated honeycomb and I had pear drop. Enjoy!" Serves 8.

Ingredients

100g plain flour

1 large egg

300ml whole milk

A little oil for frying

The Mrs Dowson's ice cream of your choice

Method

Measure your milk into a measuring jug, then break the egg into it. Mix with a fork.

Put the flour in a bowl, then make a well in the centre and pour half the milk and egg mixture into it.

Whisk together to incorporate the flour. Add the rest of the milk and egg to make a smooth thick batter. Beat to remove any lumps.

Heat a little oil in a medium frying pan or pancake pan and tip a little batter into the pan, tilting the pan as you pour, until the batter thinly coats the base.

Cook over a moderate heat for 30 seconds to a minute until golden brown on the underside.

Flip the pancake over using a palette knife or a little skill! Cook the underside again until golden brown then transfer to a plate.

Add three generous scoops of Mrs Dowson's ice cream on half of the pancake then fold over.

A taste of
HOME

Born and bred Lancastrian Nigel Barden shares food with the nation every Thursday on BBC Radio 2.

Growing up on a farm near Hawkshaw, Nigel Barden didn't have a foodie career plan and originally worked as a land agent before making the move into wine selling, then following his dream to train as an actor. He still has various strings to his bow and is a regular BBC rugby commentator as well as working as the food correspondent for BBC London.

Although he's now based near London, Nigel is still a regular visitor to Lancashire; his brother lives near Darwen and works as an accountant in Bolton and he has close links with Gibbon Bridge Hotel at Chipping near Preston.

As anyone who listens to Nigel on the Simon Mayo Show on Radio 2 knows, Nigel's a champion of local ingredients and artisan producers. And he's been able to get to know so many through his roles as chairman of judges for The Great Taste Awards, Farm Shop and Deli Awards, World Cheese Awards and the British Cookery School Awards. He also hosts the National Fish and Chip Awards.

Nigel said: "There's been a massive growth in artisan food production in the last 10 years. We've gone back to our culinary heritage and it's been a real inspiration to so many others.

"My role with The Great Taste Awards means I'm seeing the producers coming through all the time and that's a great privilege.

"In Lancashire, we have small breweries, people like Booths Supermarkets and Reg Johnson from Goosnargh Duck, who sadly passed away recently and Janet Simpson at Gibbon Bridge who champions local produce."

The link with Janet began when Nigel was a wine merchant selling to the hotel near Preston. Then, as an actor, his London-based theatre company brought a play about the Pendle Witches to Gibbon Bridge, where it was performed in view of Pendle Hill.

"I've always been in touch with Janet, and I often stage events at Gibbon Bridge," said Nigel.

"She and the team are like an extended family to me, I've known them for 30 years. Her energy's great and she's always got a plan hatching something up.

"They don't let you go – and I don't want to be let go."

Nigel Barden's
JACOB'S LADDER

Jacob's Ladder of beef is also known as short, thin or spare ribs. This recipe also works well with belly pork, which has had the rind removed. Serves 4

Ingredients

1.8kg Jacob's Ladder short rib, cut into 7½cm / 3in pieces - roughly 2 per person. Supermarkets can get it in for you, if they aren't always stocking it. This dish can also use shin of beef, oxtail or feather steak, for a similar price

120g chestnut or field mushrooms

3 fat garlic cloves

1 thumb-length (5cm) piece of ginger, or 1 tsp ground ginger

1 tsp Chinese five spice, or a mixture of ground spices (½ tsp cinnamon, ¼ tsp nutmeg and ⅛ tsp clove)

80ml of sweet or dry sherry, or rice wine

120ml soy sauce

120ml water

1 tbsp dark brown sugar

2 tsp cornflour

Method

Peel and chop the garlic, peel and slice the ginger into rounds, then mix all the ingredients apart from the cornflour and mushrooms together in a bowl and pour them over the beef.

Cover with cling film and leave for 1 hour minimum, or in the fridge overnight.

Preheat the oven to 150°C.

Remove the ribs from the fridge and put them into an ovenproof dish. Place on the hob and bring to a simmer for 5 minutes.

Remove from the hob and cover tightly with foil or a tight-fitting lid and cook in the oven for 3 hours, or longer if necessary, until the meat is tender and just falling of the bone. This could take 3-4 hours, so check every 30 minutes after 2½ hrs.

Take the ribs out of the oven and separate from the juices. Turn off the oven and cover the ribs, keeping them in the warm oven whilst you make the sauce. If any fat starts to solidify, feel free to remove it.

Pour the cooking juices through a sieve and put back into the ovenproof dish. Add 2 tablespoons of water to the cornflour to make a runny paste and add to the sauce/juices.

Add the mushrooms, sliced in half, and simmer gently for 5 minutes on the hob, over a low heat, allowing it to thicken. Season to taste.

Pour the sauce over the warm beef. Serve with rice and any green vegetables.

Not just a meal, but an ADVENTURE

Headed by celebrity chef Andrew Nutter, aided and abetted by his parents,
Nutters Restaurant prides itself on serving up a quality experience alongside
top-notch dining.

At just 16, Lancashire lad Andrew Nutter was training in the kitchens of the Savoy in London before heading off to France to further hone his skills.

Today, he's known for his TV appearances on Ready Steady Cook and his own Channel 5 show Utter Nutter – and of course the superb cuisine he serves up at Nutters Restaurant. What was once Wolstenholme Hall is now a destination restaurant set in six and a half acres of mature parkland near Rochdale.

Diners will find a menu strong on Lancashire produce with a French twist, which changes four times a year and offers daily specials and a gourmet tasting menu. The French influence isn't just found in the food, but guides Andrew's ethos of using local ingredients to their best advantage.

But he doesn't use local for local's sake. "Only if it's decent; there's no point in using it if it's inferior," said Andrew.

"We use Dingley Dell Pork from Suffolk. I've never seen such happy pigs in my life."

But lovers of Lancashire food won't be disappointed. Goosnargh poultry is on the menu cooked in dishes like duck confit with frazzled bacon, croutons and a garlic emulsion. Plus, there's Andrew's signature dish of Bury Black Pudding wontons.

Nutters is a family affair. Andrew's mum and dad greet diners and help to create an ambience that's "formal but with a kind of cosy feeling," completed by roaring fires in the winter and views across the parkland.

"Diners enjoy a great northern welcome, go to the bar to chill, ponder the menu and then through to the restaurant," said Andrew.

"People want great food and they love the family element. We like to say the Nutters experience is not just a meal but an adventure."

Nutters Restaurant

HONEY ROAST GOOSNARGH DUCK BREAST
LEG MEAT PITHIVIER & CAULIFLOWER FRITS

"Quite simply a Lancashire stunner. When you have produce of this quality you know for sure your guests are sure to enjoy. Just don't overcook the breast – the ultimate sin!" Andrew Nutter. Serves 4.

Ingredients

For the pithivier:

2 x 2kg Goosnargh ducks, legs and breast removed

2 tbsp salt

500ml goose fat

4 tbsp runny honey

1 tbsp olive oil

1 shallot and 1 clove garlic, finely chopped

25g fresh root ginger, peeled and finely chopped

4 spring onions, finely chopped

1 tbsp fresh coriander, finely chopped

180g puff pastry

1 egg yolk, to glaze

Pinch of poppy seeds

For the cauliflower frits:

20 baby cauliflower florets

Pinch curry powder

25g plain flour

1 egg, lightly beaten

25g white breadcrumbs

Vegetable oil for deep frying

For the red wine sauce:

1 shallot and 1 clove garlic, finely chopped

25ml brandy

300ml red wine

300ml strong beef stock

Method

For the leg meat pithivier

You need to start the process the night before. Take the duck legs and rub them with salt, cover and leave for at least 8 hours. Wash off the salt then place in a small roasting tray, cover with goose fat then place in a hot oven at 120°C for 2 hours 30 minutes or until tender. Cool slightly then remove all the bones.

Heat the olive oil and fry the shallot, garlic and ginger root for 2-3 minutes until softened. Remove from the heat, stir in the spring onions and coriander and leave to cool. Shred the duck leg meat, stir in and season to taste.

Form the mixture into balls the size of a golf ball. Roll out the pastry into discs 15cm in diameter, and use to encase the duck balls. Brush with egg and mark with a cocktail stick. Sprinkle with poppy seeds, then bake in a hot oven at 180°C for 15 minutes until the pastry is cooked and a light golden colour.

For the cauliflower frits

Toss the cauliflower in the curry powder, roll in the flour, then the egg and finally the breadcrumbs. Heat the oil to 180°C and deep fry until golden and crispy.

For the duck breasts

When you're ready to serve, heat a frying pan, season the duck breasts and fry fat side down until golden brown. Turn over, and seal the other side. Remove from the pan, drain off any excess fat then add the honey. Cook until a light golden colour, then spoon over the duck breasts. Place in a hot oven (180°C) and cook for 6 minutes. Remove from the oven, cover and leave to rest.

For the sauce

Return the frying pan to the heat, add the shallot and garlic and then the brandy. Flambé, stir well then add the wine and stock and reduce until about 100ml of sauce remains. Season.

To serve

Arrange the hot pithivier on serving plates, slice the duck and fan out on the plates. Spoon around the sauce and a scattering of cauliflower frits.

I serve mine with a fondant potato but alternatively use potato gratin or simply some new potatoes rolled in tarragon butter.

Love Food, LOVE PRESTON

A three-times-a-year Lancashire food market and August restaurant offers are putting Preston on the menu across the county.

Showcasing the best of Lancashire produce and organising a month-long promotion of Preston city centre's eateries, where you could find yourself dining alongside a TV star or a celebrity chef, is at the heart of Preston Business Improvement District's (BID) food agenda.

The BID was set up in 2009 to support businesses in the city centre and encourage more people to find out what's going on in Preston. A key part of that is the city's almost 100 food and hospitality businesses. Preston is ranked as one of the top 10 'restauranty' cities in the North, based on the number of eateries per head of population, and offers the full range of dining choices from chains and cafés to pubs, fine dining restaurants and unique independents.

The BID initially kicked off its foodie-focus with a celebration of Lancashire ingredients via the Lancashire Market. Preston BID manager, Mark Whittle, said: "Other places have continental markets but we thought, let's be a bit different.

"We have excellent produce around Preston, so rather than continental, we promote and celebrate fine Lancashire produce with the Lancashire Market three times a year.

"On the back of that, a lot of restaurant and eateries wanted to get involved and promote the city's love of food." In 2012,

Love Food, Love Preston was born. The month-long event offers £10 and £15 menus throughout August each year and also features 'Dine with the Stars,' where famous faces join diners for their meal.

"It gets people talking," said Mark. "But the more important message is that our restaurants are fabulous, and the £10 and £15 offers are a sweet inducement for people to try somewhere they wouldn't ordinarily go."

It's been a fantastic success for the city, especially for food businesses that have actively involved themselves in the project and promoted the Love Food, Love Preston theme to their followers on social media. As well as local people, the month-long celebration of the city's eateries regularly attracts people from around the county to see what Preston has to offer – they often then go on to be regular visitors to the city centre.

Mark said: "For too long there has been a misconception that if you want a lovely restaurant, you need to go to the coast or the countryside. "But that's not true. We've got some great brands and some great independents right here in the city centre of Preston. Whatever kind of cuisine whets your appetite, you'll find it here."

Preston (BID)
NINETEEN 75 BURY BLACK PUDDING POACHED EGG HOLLANDAISE

A tasty local black pudding treat from the Nineteen 75 restaurant.
The recipe can be easily be scaled up to feed more hungry mouths. Serves 1.

Ingredients

2 Bury black pudding slices, 1cm thick

2 slices pancetta

1 egg

Handful of rocket, washed

Balsamic glaze

For the hollandaise sauce:

250ml white wine vinegar

½ tbsp black peppercorns

2 sprigs of tarragon

2 medium egg yolks

100ml melted and skimmed butter

Squeeze of lemon juice

Method

For the hollandaise sauce

Boil the white wine vinegar, peppercorns and tarragon together and reduce by half. Strain and reserve the liquid.

Bring a quarter of a pan of water to the boil and turn the heat down to a simmer. In a heat proof bowl, whisk the egg yolks and vinegar reduction together over the simmering water until the mixture is light and fluffy.

Slowly add warmed butter, a small amount at a time, constantly whisking, until all the butter is incorporated. Mix in the lemon juice and seasoning and keep the sauce warm.

For the black pudding

Grill the black pudding and pancetta until cooked, then lightly poach the egg.

To serve

Place rocket in the centre of plate and stack a slice of black pudding then a slice of pancetta and repeat.

Top with the poached egg, coat with the Hollandaise sauce and drizzle balsamic glaze around the plate.

The Cheese FACTOR

Home to Kick Ass Cheddar and cheese celebration cakes, Procter's Cheese takes its generations of expertise in cheese making and factoring across the North.

When Tim Procter was a lad, his father was chairman of the Lancashire Cheese Factors' Association. Today, cheese factors are such a rarity, you can count the number in the whole of the UK on one hand.

"A factor buys and sells – I prefer the word factor as opposed to wholesaler – and as a cheese factor, that's all we sell," says Tim.

"We're experts who solely concentrate on one branch of produce. The remaining cheese factors don't really shout about it anymore, but I do."

Cheese expertise has been in Tim's family since the 1930s when his grandfather started making cheese at the family farm. Production was mothballed during the Second World War and started up again in the 1950s.

The factoring side of the family business, which now involves Tim's wife Sue, mother Jane and sister, Helen, began in the 1960s with his father.

"Granddad was trying to find more work for my dad and his three brothers," said Tim.

"He said to Dad: 'Why don't you go out and sell cheese?', so he put some cheese in back of his car and went out and sold it. His father said: 'Have another go tomorrow.'"

Procter's now distributes cheese from different makers to around 400 customers across the North every week – and exports to Spain - from its headquarters at Chipping in the Ribble Valley. It's also known for its spectacular multi-layered cheese celebration cakes that are built up from blocks of different varieties.

Procter's produces its own Forest of Bowland-branded cheese and Kick Ass Cheddar, a black waxed truckle cheese that is aged for 18 months and has a rich nutty flavour. It picked up its moniker when a Canadian man asked Sue for some of her 'kick ass cheddar' at a farmers' market.

Most of the cheeses factored by Procter's are from the UK and the majority are Lancashire-produced.

Tim said: "The one thing about Lancashire cheese that is absolutely unique is that it's the only type where there are three distinct, different varieties – crumbly Lancashire, creamy Lancashire and tasty Lancashire. All three are quite different."

Procter's Cheese
KICK-ASS TARTLETS

Sue Procter's own recipe for a light cheesy canapé that perfectly showcases the full flavour of Lancashire-made Kick-Ass Cheddar. Makes 12-16.

Ingredients

170g plain flour

Pinch of salt

43g margarine

43g lard

1½ tbsp water

(or cheat and use ready-made shortcrust pastry if you're in a hurry)

1 jar of Kick-Ass Hot Plum Chutney

200g truckle of Kick-Ass Cheddar – any variety can be used

Method

Sift the flour and salt into a bowl. Rub in the margarine and lard so that it resembles fine breadcrumbs. Add the water and mix to a firm dough. Chill for 15 minutes then roll out on a floured work surface.

Using a pastry cutter, cut out 12-16 rounds and place them in a greased bun tin. Prick the bases and then add a teaspoon of chutney to each one.

Place the grated Kick-Ass Cheddar on top of the chutney.

Bake at 180°C for 15-20 minutes until the cheese has melted.

Allow the tartlets to cool slightly then remove from the tin.

They're great served as canapés or with a salad for a light lunch.

A hidden gem at the centre of THE KINGDOM

Puddleducks Tea room is proud of its place on the map and the local Lancashire favourites that star on its menu.

Situated on the Duchy of Lancaster's Whitewell estate slap bang in the middle of the United Kingdom and Northern Ireland, with the Queen as Duke Of Lancaster as landlord, Puddleducks Tea room in Dunsop Bridge is more than just a café.

It's a real hub in the village, which is on the tourist map thanks to its claim to fame as the geographical centre of the UK. Puddleducks does more than just feed hungry visitors – the business is also the village post office and general store.

Tony and Glenda have been at the helm since February 2015. Former school secretary Glenda is the postmistress and Tony, an ex-operations manager is in charge of the food. Daughter Stephanie, a trained chef, is an integral part of the team.

Tony said "Cooking is a passion and for a business like ours which is seven days a week, it can't just be a job, it has to be a way of life."

Puddleducks caters for locals, tourists, walkers, cyclists and motorists exploring the Forest of Bowland which is within an Area of Outstanding Natural Beauty. Dunsop Bridge can be reached via the glorious Waddington Fell or through the breath taking Trough of Bowland, each journey magnificent in its own way. During the summer months families are seen in abundance on the village green at the front of the tea room enjoying a full day fishing and playing in the river Dunsop that runs through the village. There are also numerous lovely walks through "Dunsop Valley" and all along the river.

There is even a tarmacked walk suitable for very young children and people in wheelchairs.

At the rear of the tea room there are bike stands and a drying room for cyclists and walkers caught out by the weather. Hearty breakfasts, poached eggs and beans provide welcome high protein meals.

But Yorkshire born Tony is also a great ambassador for Lancashire favourites, including cheese and onion pie made to his own secret recipe or a hearty hotpot. Bread, cakes and scones are baked on site daily and sausages come from a local butcher. A farmer delivers bacon, pork and the ham hocks that go into Puddleducks signature dish, pea and ham soup.

"People come a long way to eat our pea and ham soup," says Tony. One customer commented; "It's so thick you could plaster a wall with it but so tasty you wouldn't try!" The traditional thick soup is available every day and Tony isn't keeping the recipe for this one secret. Turn the page to find out how to make it at home.

From October to March Puddleducks runs themed foodie nights on the first Friday of the month which have included Italian, Indian, comfort food, Tex-Mex, Spanish and Moroccan cuisines to date.

The tea room has been refurbished recently with a brand new log burner added which will match the warm welcome that awaits you at Puddleducks.

Puddleducks Tea room

Centre of the United Kingdom

Puddleducks Tea room
FAMOUS PEA AND HAM SOUP

A traditional thick, hearty and warming soup just like mother used to make.
Serves 6-8.

Ingredients

500g dried marrowfat peas

200g potatoes

1 ham hock

1 carrot, chopped

1 stick celery, chopped

1 onion, chopped

Black peppercorns

Bicarbonate of soda

Thyme

Rosemary

Sage

Bay leaf

Salt and pepper

Method

Overnight soak the ham to extract the salt and also soak the marrowfat peas in cold water with ¼ teaspoon of bicarbonate of soda.

The following day rinse both the ham hock and peas. Place the ham hock in a pan and add the carrot, celery, onion and a pinch each of sage, thyme, rosemary, one large or two small bay leaves, plus some peppercorns. Bring to the boil and simmer for 2-3 hours until the meat falls from the bones.

Cool the ham, set the stock aside, then remove the ham from the bones as well as the skin and excess fat. Shred the ham into small pieces and put to one side.

Sieve the stock and discard the vegetables. Put the stock in the fridge until you are ready to use it.

Whilst the stock is cooling and setting in the fridge, put the peas into the pan and cover to about 1 inch with cold water, and adding ¼ tsp of bicarbonate of soda. Bring to the boil and simmer until soft but not too soft – the peas should retain some texture. Remove any residue from the surface whilst the peas are simmering.

Peel and cut the potatoes into small pieces and boil in salted water until they are soft and ready to mash. Mash the potatoes using some of the stock (use a mixer with the K attachment) until you achieve a thick purée consistency. Keep to one side.

When the peas are ready, add the shredded ham, puréed mash and remaining stock. Bring to a simmer and mix until the mash is absorbed into the peas. Add salt and pepper to taste.

Serve with fresh homemade bread or a roll.

Superb steak and
QUALITY CLASSICS

A luxury B&B set in a tiny Forest of Bowland village, The Red Pump Inn is rapidly establishing itself as the place to go for steak in Lancashire.

If you're a steak-lover, The Red Pump Inn in the tiny Lancashire village of Bashall Eaves should be top of your must-visit agenda. Since being taken over by husband and wife team Jonathan and Fran Gledhill at the start of 2015, the inn has quickly earned itself a reputation as one of the top steakhouses in the North.

"Influenced by our love of provincial cuisine, our ethos is seriously good, simple food, uncomplicated while achieving great flavour through the use of top quality ingredients," says Jonathan, who in the past ran a successful steakhouse on the east coast.

The beef itself is supplied by the revered Ginger Pig of London. Native Longhorn, Shorthorn and Belted Galloway cattle mature slowly on their farms in North Yorkshire, developing a wonderful flavour as they graze on a natural diet of grass and hay. Dry aged often to over 40 days, The Red Pump is currently one of just two restaurants outside London to serve Ginger Pig steaks "attracting", says Jonathan, "everyone from our regular locals who enjoy great steak, retired farmers who really know their beef, through to those who travel some distance on word of mouth recommendation."

As well as creating a destination for steak lovers, the menu offers a delight for all foodies who just love simple dishes with superior ingredients cooked exceptionally well. Along with the Ginger Pig steaks, there are chicken, lamb and fish cuts and classics such as Fran's Irish stew and fish chowder with further specials listed daily.

Originally a small village inn, built in the 1700s, and with stunning views across the Ribble Valley to the legendary Pendle Hill, The Red Pump has had new life and character injected by the bucket load. With an elegantly rural interior, stone flag floors, oak beams, crackling open fires, eight boutique B&B bedrooms with French antique beds and wet room showers, and this year they've introduced luxury glamping yurts complete with en-suite and log burning stove!

Recommended in Alastair Sawday's Secret Places and the Good Pub Guide, travellers who appreciate the relaxed and informal luxury often leave reviews paying tribute to the warm Irish hospitality exuded by Fran, who originally hails from Kildare and let's not forget the Irish breakfast – the full English plus white pudding and soda bread.

"We care passionately," says Fran "about providing a genuine, warm, heartfelt welcome into our home for all our guests and are motivated by the love for what we do and the quality of the product we provide."

THE RED
PUMP INN

BASHALL EAVES

...Seriously Good

The Red Pump Inn
PRIME RIB STEAK AND CHIMICHURRI SAUCE

The prime rib or côte de boeuf as it's referred to in France, is a big piece of incredibly tasty prime steak meat left on the bone. The best example will be from a native slow growing grass fed beast and dry aged for at least 40 days. Serve with an Argentine chimichurri sauce. Serving size will depend on how big your prime rib is.

Ingredients

For the chimichurri

2 handfuls of parsley, the freshest you can find

4 cloves garlic

2 handfuls coriander

1½ tbsp red chilli flakes

Extra virgin olive oil

Balsamic vinegar

For the steak

1 large prime rib steak on the bone

Rapeseed oil

Olive oil

Butter

Sea salt and freshly ground black pepper

Method

For the chimichurri

Make the chimichurri in advance. You can leave the sauce to do its thing overnight, as the flavour will intensify the longer it sits. At least a week is usually good. Chop, dice, mince or pound the garlic and herbs to your preferred texture. You can use a food processor or big knife.

Add the red chilli flakes, olive oil, and vinegar, and stir it all together until well blended.

For the steak

Remove the steak from the fridge at least 30 minutes before cooking and bring up to room temperature, to allow the meat to cook more evenly and ensure it's tender and juicy.

Trim off all excess fat around the rib end to expose the bone (this gives you something to hold onto when you're gnawing on it).

Light your chargrill/barbeque/fire pit or oven (this beast is too big to cook completely on the grill). Ensuring it's hot, at least 200°C.

Brush the steak with a little oil (we use rapeseed) and season generously with sea salt flakes and freshly ground coarse black pepper.

Place the steak on the grill bars, presentation side down, and cook for 2-3 minutes. Only move if it's flaming excessively.

Rotate the steak through 90° to achieve the crossed branding marks and cook for another couple of minutes.

Turn the steak over and cook for a further 3-4 minutes.

Preheat a heavy pan and add a little oil and small knob of butter. Once the butter foams, place the steak into the centre of the pan. Pop into the oven for 8-10 minutes. Finishing in the oven gives the steak a perfectly even caramelised crust while remaining succulent and juicy.

Remove the steak from the oven and allow it to rest for a good 10 minutes. This dish doesn't have to be served piping hot; it's more important to get all those lovely juices flowing internally. Now pour yourself a glass of Malbec and don't poke, slice or touch the steak until rested.

Transfer the steak to a cutting board and slice into thick hunky pieces.

To serve

Serve the steak and chimichurri with French fries and what's left of that bottle of the Malbec. Share only with your very dearest friends!

So much more than jam and
JERUSALEM

Cakes to Caribbean cookery are on the foodie fundraising agenda for the Saddleworth WI.

Mention the Women's Institute to many people, and jam making is the first thing that comes to mind.

But Saddleworth WI, which has been running in its latest incarnation for eight years "isn't that kind of WI", according to its president Jess Moreland.

Jess, who makes cakes rather than jam, said: "It would be nice to try to change that image. The WI is a massive part of our British heritage but it's not all blue rinses and bad knitwear, which the WI is commonly mistaken for."

Saddleworth WI, which draws in women from five local villages and meets monthly at the Saddleworth Hotel, has 100 members aged between 25 and 85. It's a very foodie branch that's known for the fabulous cakes that members make.

Local people have a chance to sample them when they are sold at WI fundraisers throughout the year, notably the popular annual Christmas markets at the Saddleworth Hotel, where the members' stall includes the 'legendary' offerings from the Little Saddleworth Pie Company and Spread the Love preserves and chutneys.

Jess said: "There are some very keen bakers in our WI, which is one of the biggest WI's in the country.

"Food does make up a big part of it, mainly cakes. We have introduced a food hall to the Christmas markets, due to massive demand and we raise funds for a different local charity every year."

Foodie fundraising efforts have included cake baking, country fairs, afternoon tea at a member's house and even a Caribbean barbeque.

Saddleworth WI is a keen supporter of local Lancashire food too, and the food and drink subgroup visits a different local restaurant, café or bar every month. The monthly Crafty Cake subgroup also meets at local artisan café Scona at Reclamation Rooms to learn and teach various crafts, accompanied by a bring and share cake session, washed down with lattés.

Jess said: "We want to encourage women to expand their social and educational mindset. The WI can be informative, inspirational and really good fun. It's a big deal in some women's lives – for some it's a lifesaver."

Saddleworth WI
BANANA AND PECAN LOAF

A tasty teatime treat to use up your very ripe bananas that's surprisingly quick and easy to make. Serves 8-10.

Ingredients

225g self-raising flour
1 tsp baking powder
112g sugar
75g margarine
1 large egg
3 medium bananas, going black and spotty (this is essential)
112g pecan nuts, chopped
2-3 tbsp Demerara sugar

Method

Preheat the oven to 180°C.

Sieve the flour and baking powder into a mixing bowl. Add the sugar, egg and margarine to the flour. Blend together with an electric mixer to a breadcrumb consistency.

Place the peeled bananas into a separate bowl and mash with a potato masher or fork. Add the squashed banana and chopped pecans into the bowl with the other ingredients.

Mix all together to a smooth consistency and pour into a 900g loaf baking tin. Level off with a spoon so the mixture is flat.

Sprinkle the Demerara sugar across the top of the cake mix in the tin, then bake in the centre of the oven for 50 minutes.

When cooked, cool on a rack, slice and enjoy with a mug of tea.

Note: Storing in a Tupperware box tends to make this loaf damp and squishy, thanks to the moisture from the bananas. The loaf stays firmer and easier to cut when wrapped and stored in greaseproof baking paper.

A feast for the eyes and the
TASTEBUDS

Home-produced honey, herbs, vegetables and eggs take centre stage at stunning stately home Samlesbury Hall's restaurant.

When Samlesbury Hall near Preston was built in the 14th century, it was a self-sufficient estate feeding the family and their servants with ingredients sourced from its own land.

Fast-forward seven centuries, and you might be surprised to learn that just like the lords of old, when you eat at Samlesbury Hall today many of the ingredients come from its own gardens.

"We grow our own vegetables and herbs, and you often see chefs running across the courtyard for some mint," said hall director, Sharon Jones.

"We've reintroduced historic medicinal and culinary plants for use in the kitchens, and we save ex-battery hens. They are loose in the grounds and we use their eggs."

Honey comes from the hall's bee centre, which has five hives containing 50,000 bees. They are traditional British black bees, which Sharon – a beekeeper herself - says aren't as productive as the more common Italian varieties but are "so much nicer."

Ice cream served in the restaurant and ice cream parlour is made from milk produced by cows grazing in the adjoining field. Meat comes from the local butcher who sources Forest of Bowland lamb, beef, pork, poultry and sausages, and seafood makes the short journey from Fleetwood. The hall has its own label merlot, too.

"We're very much into keeping things within the county," says Sharon.

It's a successful policy that has earned Samlesbury Hall Taste Lancashire's highest quality accreditation for five years running.

The restaurant specialises in traditional British food and Sunday lunches, in what was once a Victorian billiards room furnished with vintage chairs and tables. All meals are freshly-made and the restaurant is renowned for its Lancashire hotpot and dishes such as a duo of pork on grainy mash, ham hock terrine, black pudding bubble and squeak and its homemade pâté.

The seasonal menu changes twice a year and the "splendid" afternoon teas have really caught customers' imagination. Also look out for the wafflery, crêperie and ice-cream parlour.

Although the hall is a visual feast with a free entry policy, Sharon admits: "We usually have more people coming for the restaurant than to look around the hall!"

Samlesbury Hall

TWICE-COOKED CONFIT OF DUCK WITH RABENDA JUS

A flavoursome duck dish with added depth from the red wine jus that's perfect for a dinner party or posh supper. Serves 4.

Ingredients

For the duck:

4 duck legs

50g ginger root, roughly chopped

Large garlic bulb, chopped

1 white onion, sliced

10 peppercorns

25g salt

25g Chinese five spice powder

5 juniper berries

Vegetable oil

For the jus:

50ml red wine

50ml ruby Port

25g honey

100ml beef stock

2 stalks fresh lavender

Salt to taste

50g tomato paste

25g butter

Method

For the duck

Place the duck, skin side up, in a medium-sized ovenproof dish. Add a little of the vegetable oil to a frying pan and gently fry the onion, garlic and ginger until fragrant (about 2-3 minutes) and add to the duck.

Add the rest of the ingredients to the dish and cover with vegetable oil.

Cover the dish with tin foil and cook in a preheated oven at 140°C for 3 hours.

Once tender allow the duck to cool in the oil overnight.

For the jus

Add the red wine and Port to a saucepan, bring to a boil and reduce by half. Once reduced, add the rest of the ingredients apart from the butter and bring to the boil again; the tomato paste and honey will thicken the sauce slightly.

To serve

When ready to serve, remove the duck legs from the oil and debone, place on a baking tray, skin side up, and cook in the oven at 220°C until the skin is darkened and crisp.

Heat up the jus and once simmering, remove from heat and whisk in the butter.

We serve our duck on a red onion and cucumber salad, and garnish with some julienne leeks fried in oil until crispy, with a drizzle of jus over the duck and plate.

Samlesbury Hall
ROASTED MEDITERRANEAN VEGETABLES

A super dish for vegetarians; replace the paneer with tofu for a vegan version
or add chicken or fish if you're a meat eater. Serves 2.

Ingredients

450ml boiling water

100g basmati rice

1 bell pepper

½ red onion

1 clove garlic, finely chopped

1 courgette

1 tsp fresh coriander, chopped

6 asparagus spears

40g fine beans

20g sugar snap peas

200g paneer cheese (or tofu if vegan)

80g sun-blush tomatoes

2 tbsp sun-blush tomato oil for marinade

Olive oil

Balsamic vinegar

Salt and black pepper

Method

Roughly chop the peppers, onion, courgette and paneer cheese into a bowl. Add the sun-blush oil, fine beans, sugar snap peas, garlic and asparagus spears and mix together so that all of the ingredients are coated in oil. Leave to stand for one hour in the fridge.

Cook the rice in boiling water for approximately 10 minutes. Drain and rinse in cold water and tightly pack into two ramekins (90cm wide and 45cm deep). The rice is now ready for the microwave. If you prefer, you can mix the rice with chopped coriander before potting up.

In a red hot griddle pan, sear a couple of handfuls of the vegetable mix for approximately 1½ minutes for each batch, to colour and flavour. Tip out onto a baking tray ready to finish in the oven. The vegetables can now be left until you are ready to eat.

To finish off the dish, add sun-blush tomatoes to the vegetables and season with salt and black pepper. Place in the oven at 180°C for around 5 minutes depending on how crunchy you like your vegetables. Microwave the rice to heat through.

To serve

Tip the ramekin of rice onto a serving plate, leaving the ramekin on until you have plated-up the vegetables. Toss over the chopped coriander and drizzle with olive oil and balsamic vinegar to serve.

A Master CHEF

Local ingredients and educating the next generation are top of the agenda for MasterChef 2015 winner Simon Wood.

The foundations for Simon Wood's cookery career, which has taken him from TV to executive chef at Oldham Athletic, were laid in his grandma's kitchen.

"I loved baking and cooking with my grandma," he says.

"But when I was with her, we'd do different things like rabbit stew, things that we didn't have at home. I enjoyed going there at the weekend – baking, then going to cinema and coming home and eating the things we'd prepared.

"Food has always been associated with family and I've done that with my kids too; starting baking when they were little and having dinner together. Creating happy memories with food is something I enjoy – I guess that's why I do it really."

Simon, from Chadderton, creates three seasonal menus throughout the year for diners at Oldham Athletic and also showcases his skills at food festivals. The best ingredients, he says, are the ones he sources locally, and he's a big supporter of the farm to fork philosophy.

"I used my local, Albion farm shop near Saddleworth, a lot. It's a place I go regularly," said Simon.

"The products they have are unbelievable; you can't go wrong. The meat is great, the bacon and belly pork you get there are astonishing, it's so good and I think I've used it on every menu I've created. If you go to your local farm shop, you know where it's come from."

Provenance is important to Simon, and he believes many health problems can be tackled with a little bit of education about what we put on our plates.

"Obesity, diabetes – it's all linked back to what you put in," he says.

"Diet is a really vital thing in health and wellbeing, especially in kids. I'm not a fan of sauces in jars and gravy granules. There isn't much in those things that you can't make at home. A pasta sauce doesn't take much time to knock-up, and you know what's in there and what you're giving your family and friends."

And most of it can be sourced from Lancashire.

"Absolutely," says Simon. "We've got really good produce. You won't have to go anywhere else again."

See more of Simon's recipes in his book: At Home With Simon Wood – Fine Dining Made Simple available from Amazon and Waterstones.

Simon Wood's
PORK BELLY WITH MARVELLOUS MASH, BROAD BEANS AND ASPARAGUS

You will need to do this the day before so that you can press and portion it.
Serves 4.

Ingredients

100g pork belly per person

For the marvellous mash:

1kg red potatoes, peeled, cubed

100ml double cream

400g unsalted butter, diced

Sea salt

White pepper

For the broad beans and asparagus:

50g broad beans

3 asparagus spears per person

Iced water

Method

For the pork belly

Preheat the oven to 150°C. On a wire rack over a baking tray slowly roast the belly pork for 4½ hours. Alternatively you can sous vide the pork at 82°C for 18 hours, I find this provides the best result.

Once the pork belly is cooked lay it between two pieces of baking paper and press between two baking trays. Weigh it down (I use tins from my cupboard) and then chill in the fridge overnight. The next day you can remove the jellified stock that collects in the tray and set aside in a small saucepan. Reduce this over a high heat before serving with your finished dish.

Next portion the pork neatly before gently pan frying until golden on all sides ready for service.

For the marvellous mash

Boil the potatoes in well salted water until soft. Drain over the sink in a colander and then place a clean tea towel over the top. This will draw any moisture into it leaving you with fluffy, steamed dry potatoes.

In a saucepan on a low heat add the cream and butter, 1½ teaspoons of sea salt and a really good twist of white pepper and gently melt.

If you have a ricer pass your potato through it onto a saucepan over a very low heat. Now start to ladle your mixture one ladle at a time onto your potato, whisking until incorporated. Check your seasoning and set aside.

For the broad beans and asparagus:

Peel the broad beans and stems of asparagus.

Fill a large saucepan with water, season well and bring it to the boil. Add the broad beans and asparagus and cook for 1 minute. Immediately add into the iced water to stop the cooking process and stir them around to ensure even cooling. Once cool remove and dry on kitchen paper or a J-cloth. To serve, add a little butter to a frying pan, season with salt and then heat through.

To plate

Pipe the mash to get a good presentation style; it can be hot so pop some gloves on if needed. Plate the sliced pork belly alongside the mash, finish with your greens and reduced stock then serve immediately.

See more of Simon's recipes in his book: At Home With Simon Wood - Fine Dining Made Simple available from Amazon and Waterstones.

The perfect excuse to INDULGE

A contemporary take on afternoon tea is turning The Village Tea Room at Wheelton into a must-visit destination for fans of a warm welcome and fine baking.

Local husband and wife team, Martyn and Jackie Connor, welcome you to The Village Tea Room at Wheelton, a family-run tea room located in front of the beautiful clock tower memorial in the quaint village of Wheelton, near Chorley.

Part of the village borders the Leeds and Liverpool canal and the immediate surroundings are a hive of activity during the summer months as the narrow boats ply their way along this pleasant stretch of the canal.

Since opening in August 2015 the tea room has become a real community hub attracting customers locally and from all corners of Lancashire.

Martyn and Jackie have a passion to provide friendly service, in modern and elegant surroundings, serving up quality homemade food at affordable prices and ensuring that you enjoy your experience whilst in their company.

Their menu is freshly prepared on a daily basis, offering a simple but varied selection of light lunches and sweet and savoury delights, complemented with a range of dairy and gluten-free products.

"We are really excited to offer our customers a unique and special experience when they visit The Village Tea Room at Wheelton for that special afternoon tea occasion," said Martyn and Jackie

Their signature offering is a unique 'picnic basket afternoon tea' which offers a selection of freshly prepared finger sandwiches, a shot of soup, a selection of mini cakes and a scone with jam and clotted cream, all served with a choice of tea, coffee or a soft drink.

Whether you are visiting for a special indulgent treat or to celebrate a special event such as a birthday, a pre-wedding or baby shower party with a group of friends, then the 'picnic basket afternoon tea' complements that occasion perfectly.

Their cakes, pastries, biscuits and desserts are only ever homemade using free-range eggs and the best butter. Fresh scones are freshly baked every day by Jackie and her team in the open-plan kitchen, perfectly designed so that you can see at close hand how your food is carefully and lovingly prepared by their experienced team.

The most important ingredients to serve up a delightful and flavoursome range of homemade cakes and pastries are the milk and cream, provided by John and Karen, the local farmers at the Denham Springs Dairy not a mile away from the tea rooms and a beautiful location. The free-range eggs are also locally supplied by Staveleys of Coppull.

"Lancashire-sourced produce and product are very important to us but if we do stray into neighbouring counties, it's only to bring our customers great products at affordable prices such as our Hawkshead Relish ranges from the Lake District and our Taylors of Harrogate tea and coffee from Yorkshire," explains Martyn.

"From our perspective we would love to become our customers perfect excuse for an enjoyable treat with family or friends," they said.

The Village Tea room at Wheelton

Today's Specials

Soup of the Day

Courgette & Pepper
or Mushroom
£3.95

Hot Dish of the Day

Cheese & Onion Pie
served with salad, baked
beans or mushy peas
£4.85

Quiche of the Day

Cheese & Pepper
served with salad, baked
beans or mushy peas
£4.85

...and for Dessert

The Village Tea Room at Wheelton
CLASSIC FRUIT SCONES

This is the scone that's an integral part of The Village Tea Room's yummy wicker basket afternoon teas. Makes 12.

Ingredients

Ingredients

500g self-raising flour

125g butter, cut into cubes

75g caster sugar

110g sultanas (reduce to 55g if you're making 6 fruit and 6 plain scones)

2 medium free-range eggs

118ml milk

¼ tsp baking powder

Strawberry jam and clotted cream, to serve

Method

Place all the flour and sugar into a large mixing bowl and add the baking powder. Add the butter, then rub in with your fingers until the mix looks like fine breadcrumbs.

Make a well in the dry mix, then add the milk and eggs and combine it quickly with your hands to the required consistency. Add the sultanas and mix in.

Scatter some flour onto your work surface and tip the dough out. Dredge the dough and your hands with more flour, then fold the dough over 2-3 times until its smoother. Pat into a round, about 2cm deep.

Use a 5cm cutter and dip it into some flour. Plunge the cutter into the dough and repeat until you have four scones. Then press what's left of the dough back into a round to cut out another four.

Repeat until you have used up your mixture, then carefully place close together on a parchment-lined baking tray in rows.

Bake at 165°C for 15 minutes until risen and golden on the top.

Serve with strawberry jam and clotted cream.

Stand and DELIVER

Real food and real ales are at the heart of the White Horse, an 18th century pub with a 21st century outlook.

Originally a highwayman's pub and one of the first buildings at the crossroads in Edgworth, The White Horse has been through some major changes since it was built in 1790.

While the listed building retains plenty of its original features – although the highwaymen are long gone – there's been a big shake up since managing director Alex Dickenson took over the traditional country pub in 2013. As well as top to toe refurbishment, a new kitchen team was a big part of the investment.

"Our head chef Gary has been in the trade for 30 years in gastropubs, fine dining and hotels," says Alex.

"He wanted to come to a country pub doing fresh food from scratch, with an English twist."

The White Horse prides itself in offering something for everyone, with Lancashire ingredients at the centre of each dish, and a specials board that changes weekly.

Alex said: "All our meat comes from our butcher, who is five miles down the road, the vegetables are from Bolton and fish from Fleetwood comes in daily. The fish and chips you'd eat tonight would have been delivered this morning."

The beer battered fish and chips are a big hit and the pub runs a chippy tea night on Thursdays. The menu ranges from basics to gastropub dishes, and there is plenty of choice behind the bar for real ale fans with rotating guest beers a big draw for drinkers.

Alex, from a former country house management background is keen to ring in the changes wherever possible.

"I go mystery shopping once a week to see what we could do differently," he said.

"We're always thinking of new ideas to keep with the times – that's what hospitality is all about."

But at the same time, he wants to keep the local, traditional ambience of the pub, with good food, drink and service at the top of the menu.

"There's nothing better than sitting by the fire on a cold winter's day with a well-kept pint of real ale and a really good English dish," he said.

The White Horse
STUFFED FREE-RANGE CHICKEN

With Blacksticks Blue Cheese and Bury black pudding, topped with a wild mushroom and shallot sauce, and served on a bed of crushed buttered Jersey Royal potatoes. Serves 1, but easily scalable.

Ingredients

250g free-range local chicken breast

25g Blacksticks Blue cheese

25g Bury black pudding

2 slices (approx 20g) slices Parma ham

75g fresh wild mushrooms

50g shallots

125ml white wine

100ml double cream

4 strands (approx 4g) fresh chives, chopped

Pinch of salt and pepper for seasoning

50g butter

150g Jersey Royal potatoes

Pea shoots, for garnish

Method

For the chicken

Butterfly the chicken breast to open it up and breast-side down. Place half of the Blacksticks Blue in the centre of the chicken breast.

Slice the black pudding into four pieces and place on top of the cheese, then place the remaining cheese on top of the black pudding. Fold back the chicken so its face side up.

Wrap the Parma ham around the chicken evenly, so it covers it all the way around the middle.

Lay a long piece of cling film on top of your work top, sit the chicken in the centre then roll the cling film around the chicken.

In order to compact the chicken in the centre, you now need to tie one end of cling film, and then push the chicken towards the tied end to create a roll. Twist the cling-filmed parcel until it's tight at both ends.

Place the parcel on a piece of tin foil and roll into a sausage shape, twisting both ends again to retain the shape of the chicken.

Place into a pan of water and simmer gently for approximately 25 minutes.

Boil a pan of cold water and cook the Jersey Royals for approximately 20 minutes until soft. Strain off all the water, add half the butter and a pinch of salt and pepper for seasoning, then crush the potatoes with the chopped chives.

For the sauce

Place the rest of the butter in a heavy-based saucepan, add the shallots and cook for 3–4 minutes.

Add the mushrooms and cook for a further two minutes. Add the wine and cream, then reduce by half. Check the seasoning.

To serve

Carefully unwrap chicken, cut in half and place on top of the crushed potatoes.

Spoon the sauce around the base of a dinner plate.

Garnish with fresh chives or pea shoots.

Destination: LANCASHIRE

Boasting a head chef who cooked at Claridge's and the Savoy Grill, The Yew Tree Inn Anglezarke provides a relaxed gastropub experience served up with local ingredients.

High-quality local produce served in a relaxed atmosphere has put The Yew Tree Inn Anglezarke on the map as a destination Lancashire gastropub.

Specialising in modern British cuisine, with highlights including braised beef short rib, plus stupendous Sunday lunches, the inn offers a seasonal menu that makes the most of ingredients at their best.

Greg Armstrong, who co-runs the pub with Ben Wheale, said: "Everything is as local as possible. We go to suppliers and speak to them directly and build up relationships.

"There is a very short distance from farm to table; we are very rural and surrounded by farms. If you're on the terrace outside, the cows come up to the glass wall surrounding you."

The menus are the creation of head chef Oliver Farrar, who boasts a CV that includes Claridge's Hotel and the Savoy Grill. He has plenty of top class ingredients to play with when putting together both the seasonal menus and weekly specials. As well as great local meat and vegetables, The Yew Tree buys its cheeses from Pat's Cheese Stall at Chorley market.

Dating back to 1871, the inn has a rural feel, with original exposed beams, flagstone floors, oak furniture and touches of tweed designed to provide a comfortable ambience for diners. Special food-based evening events and live music are also regularly on the menu.

"We get local trade but we're becoming known as a destination restaurant throughout Lancashire," said Greg.

Although he describes the pub as "completely food-led," diners can also enjoy Lancashire-brewed ales from the Rivington and Blackedge breweries at the bar as well as a comprehensive selection of gins.

"The beers are very local – two of our beers are literally brewed 200 yards away and the other brewery is less than 10 minutes from the inn," said Greg.

The Yew Tree Inn Anglezarke certainly ticks all the boxes if you're looking for a proper taste of Lancashire.

The Yew Tree Inn Anglezarke

RICOTTA WITH BALSAMIC GLAZE, DRIED HERBS AND SOURDOUGH BREAD

A completely homemade artisan treat of a platter that you'll savour all the more because of the love that's gone into making it. Serves 6.

Ingredients

For the sourdough:

600g – 1kg strong white bread flour for the starter dough

300g strong white bread flour for the sponge

100g sourdough starter

For the ricotta:

1 litre whole milk

600ml double cream

18g Maldon sea salt

40ml lemon juice

26ml white wine vinegar

For the balsamic glaze:

250ml balsamic vinegar

125g soft dark brown sugar

For the dried herbs:

½ bunch thyme

½ bunch rosemary

Sea salt

Method

For the sourdough

You need to do this the day before. To make the starter, combine 200g flour with 200ml lukewarm water in a container and leave somewhere warm, uncovered, overnight.

The following day, feed it by discarding half and adding 100g flour and 100ml lukewarm water. Feed daily until you see bubbles throughout the mixture. It takes a few days for the mixture to pick up the natural airborne yeasts.

Remove 100g of the starter for your loaf, chill the rest. Feed this once a week by bringing to room temperature, allowing it to bubble and then recede somewhere warm for 30 minutes to an hour. Return to the fridge.

To make the sponge, bring 100g of starter to room temperature. Combine the flour and ½ tsp of sea salt in a bowl, then add 300ml of warm water.

Cover with a towel and leave it double in size somewhere warm for 3-4 hours.

To make the sourdough bread

Combine the sponge with the flour, 2tsp of salt, then turn out onto a floured surface.

Knead for 10 minutes until smooth and elastic. Place in a lightly oiled bowl, cover and leave to double in size in a warm place for 2-3 hours.

Preheat the oven to 220°C.

Place a tray of water in the base of the oven (this helps develop a good crust). Score the top of the loaf with a sharp knife. Bake for 30-40 minutes until golden and it sounds hollow when tapped. Cool on a wire rack.

For the ricotta

Bring the milk, cream and salt to boil in a large pan, whisking occasionally to stop it scalding the bottom.

When simmering, add lemon juice and vinegar and whisk. Remove from the heat and cool to room temperature for about an hour.

Line a large flat tray with muslin cloth. Ladle the large curds out of the pan into the muslin. Discard the liquid. Fold the muslin over the cheese and cling film the tray. Drain overnight.

For the balsamic glaze

Mix the vinegar and sugar in a saucepan over a medium heat, stirring constantly until the sugar dissolves.

Bring to the boil, reduce the heat and reduce the mixture by half until it coats the back of a spoon (approximately 20 minutes).

For the dried herbs

Strip the herbs from the stalks. Bake on a tray at 150°C for 5 minutes. Cool and break down to an almost crumb consistency.

The Yew Tree Inn Anglezarke
PAN-ROAST LAMB CANON

Served with a delicious mix of red and spring cabbage, parsley root purée and black pudding hash browns. Serves 4.

Ingredients

For the lamb and lamb sauce:

1 lamb loin

1 garlic clove and 1 sprig thyme

50g salted butter

3 tbsp plain flour

100ml Port

1 litre chicken stock

500g lamb bones

For the parsley root purée:

3 parsley roots

100ml each of whole milk and double cream

20g salted butter

For the red cabbage purée:

½ red cabbage

200m each of red wine and apple juice

1 star anise and 1 cinnamon stick

50ml balsamic vinegar

For the spring cabbage

1 spring cabbage

20g parsley, chopped

10g salted butter

For the Jerusalem artichokes

500g Jerusalem artichokes

50ml each of olive oil

50ml white wine vinegar

2 cloves garlic and 2 bay leaves

For the black pudding hash browns

40g black pudding

6 King Edward potatoes

50ml olive oil

Method

For the lamb

Season the lamb loin with salt and pepper and cut in half.

Colour the loin evenly in a hot frying pan. Add the butter, garlic and thyme. Monitoring the heat so that the butter doesn't burn, then baste the lamb for approximately 5 minutes.

Remove from the pan and allow to rest. Once ready to serve place, on a tray in a 200°C oven for 3 minutes.

For the lamb sauce

In a hot saucepan, caramelise the lamb bones. Once nicely coloured, pour in the Port to deglaze the pan. Cook until the port has reduced to a syrup then add the chicken stock.

Bring to the boil and simmer for 30-40 minutes. Strain the bones and return the liquid to the heat. Reduce by one-third then whisk in the flour. Strain and put aside.

For the parsley root purée

Peel and roughly dice the parsley roots. Place in a saucepan and cover with the butter and milk. Bring to the boil then simmer for 20-30 minutes until soft.

Strain and place in a food processor with the butter. Blend until smooth and season with salt.

For the red cabbage purée

Thinly slice the cabbage and place in a saucepan with the rest of the ingredients.

Bring to the boil and simmer for 40-45 minutes until tender. Once cooked, remove the star anise and cinnamon stick. Place the cabbage and remaining liquid into a food processor then blend until smooth. Season with salt.

For the spring cabbage

Thinly shred the cabbage ensuring the root has been removed. Cook in salted boiling water for 2 minutes.

Strain and return to a dry saucepan with the butter. Ensure the butter melts through the cabbage then add the chopped parsley and salt to taste.

For the Jerusalem artichokes

Peel the artichokes then cut into chunks. Using a frying pan, add oil and gently fry on a medium heat until golden, add a bay leaves, garlic, and a splash of white wine vinegar.

Place on a lid for 25 minutes to soften.

For the black pudding hash brown

Wash the potatoes and cover with water in a pan. Bring to the boil then simmer for 10 minutes. Strain.

Once the potatoes have cooled slightly, peel, then grate with a coarse grater.

Season the potato mix then pack into 2 cooking rings until half way up. Add 20g black pudding to each ring, then fill up with the remaining potato and compress until tight.

Push the hash browns from the moulds and fry in hot oil until golden. Bake in the oven at 180°C for 10 minutes, remove and slice in half through the centre.

The Yew Tree Inn Anglezarke
BLOOD ORANGE CHEESECAKE

A zesty pudding that's made extra special with homemade sorbet and orange crisps. Serves 12.

Ingredients

For the cheesecake base:

100g digestive biscuits

50g Demerara sugar

50g melted butter

For the filling:

500g full fat cream cheese

100g icing sugar

1 vanilla pod, sliced lengthways, or 1 tsp vanilla extract

200ml double cream, lightly whipped

2 blood oranges, juiced and zested

For the topping:

250ml blood orange juice or purée

3 leaves gelatine

For the sorbet:

200g caster sugar

600ml blood orange juice

½ lemon, juiced

2 tbsp Amaretto

For the orange crisps:

1 blood orange

Icing sugar

Method

For the cheesecake base

Place the digestives in a food processer and pulse until crumbed. Tip out into a bowl and mix in the sugar and butter.

Once well mixed, spoon the mixture into a 20cm spring-form cake tin lined with baking parchment. Use a metal spoon to press the biscuit crumbs down firmly and evenly. Chill in the fridge until set.

For the filling

In a large mixing bowl, using a whisk or a wooden spoon, beat together the cream cheese, icing sugar and vanilla pod seeds or vanilla extract until well mixed.

Fold in the double cream, mixing well. Once incorporated, fold in the blood orange juice and zest.

Spoon the cream cheese mixture over the chilled biscuit base, making sure that there are no air bubbles. Smooth the top of the cheesecake with a palette knife or metal spoon.

Place in the fridge for 1 hour until set.

For the topping

Soak the gelatine in cold water.

Bring the orange juice or purée to the boil then whisk in the softened gelatine.

Cool to room temperature before pouring on top of the cheesecake and allow to set for 1 hour before removing the cheesecake from the mould.

For the sorbet

Place the sugar and 150ml water in a small pan and simmer for 5-10 minutes until syrupy. Remove from the heat and cool.

Stir the orange and lemon juice and the Amaretto into the syrup. Pour into an ice cream machine and churn according to the manufacturer's instructions (or pour into a plastic container, cover with a lid, chill for 1 hour, then whisk every 30 minutes for 2 hours to break up the ice crystals). Freeze until firm.

For the orange crisps

Slice the blood orange as thinly as you can then dust each side with the icing sugar. Lay the slices onto parchment paper then place in a 150°C oven.

After 30 minutes turn the slices over, then allow to dry for a further 30 minutes. Remove from the oven and allow to firm up.

The DIRECTORY

These great businesses have supported the making of this book; please support and enjoy them.

Albion Farm Shop
Oldham Road,
Delph,
Saddleworth,
OL35RQ
Telephone: 01457 874366
Website: www.albionfarmshop.co.uk
Family-owned and run farm shop and café, selling and serving a huge range of local produce, including beef and lamb from its own fields.

Barrique
3 Market Hall,
Lytham,
Lancashire, FY8 5LW
Telephone: 01253 736 877
Website: www.barriquelytham.com
Wine shop, deli and bar with small tapas and a superb selection of gins, offering the chance to explore wine and enjoy taste.

Barton Grange Garden Centre
Garstang Road,
Brock,
Preston,
Lancashire, PR3 0BT
Tel: 01995 642900
Website: www.bartongrange.co.uk
Award-winning garden centre, farm shop, restaurant and café with a focus on Lancashire produce.

Bashall Barn
Bashall Town,
Clitheroe,
Lancashire BB7 3LQ
Telephone: 01200 428 964
Website: www.bashallbarn.co.uk
Farm shop, restaurant, café, ice cream parlour and wedding venue specialising in homemade food from local produce.

Bertram's Restaurant
Crow Wood,
Royle Lane,
Off Holme Road,
Burnley,
Lancashire, BB12 0RT
Telephone: 01282 471930
Website: www.bertramsrestaurant.com
Destination restaurant set within an award-winning spa, with over-16s entry policy for adult-only dining.

The Bird at Birtle
239 Bury And Rochdale Old Road,
Birtle,
Lancashire, OL10 4BQ
Gastropub run by celebrity chef Andrew Nutter with a focus on Lancashire produce, serving cask ales and regionally-inspired dishes.

The Blue Mallard

Burscough Wharf,

Liverpool Road,

North, Burscough, L40 5RZ

Telephone: 01704 893954

Website: thebluemallard.co.uk

The Blue Mallard located at Burscough Wharf; a unique, canalside development in the heart of Burscough town centre. The restaurant is run by Head Chef Chris, a local lad who is passionate about great food and top-rate dining.

Brown's the Butchers

7 Market Place,

Chorley,

Lancashire, PR7 1DA

Telephone: 01257 276515

Website:

www.brownsthebutchers.co.uk and

www.lancashirehaggis.co.uk

Family-run butchers, supplying locally-sourced meat and the home of the English haggis.

Bury Black Pudding Company

Units 12-14, J2 Business Park

Bridgehall Lane

Bury BL9 7NY

Telephone: 0161 797 0689

Website:

www.buryblackpuddings.co.uk

The finest award-winning black puddings made in Bury.

Butler's Farmhouse Cheeses

Shay Lane Industrial Estate,

Shay Lane,

Longridge,

Preston,

Lancashire, PR3 3BT

Telephone: 01772 781500

Website: www.butlerscheeses.co.uk

Home of the famous Blacksticks Blue and a selection of cow and goats' milk cheeses, handmade from milk from the family own herds and local suppliers.

Capri

4a Dicconson Terrace

Lytham

Lancashire, FY8 5JY

Telephone: 01253 735034

Website: www.caprilytham.com

A Mediterranean-style café and bar open from 8am until late, with pasta, pizzas and ice cream made on the premises, and a fantastic cocktail menu.

The Cartford Inn and TOTI Deli

The Cartford Inn,

Cartford Lane,

Little Eccleston,

Lancashire, PR3 0YP

Telephone: 01995 670166

Website: www.thecartfordinn.co.uk

Email: info@thecartfordinn.co.uk

Facebook: TheCartfordInn

Instagram: @cartfordinn

Twitter: @cartfordinn

17th century coaching inn turned gastropub and boutique hotel, with on-site deli offering a 'taste of the inn'.

Cowman's Famous Sausage Shop

13 Castle Street,

Clitheroe,

Lancashire, BB7 2BT

Telephone: 01200 423842

Website: www.cowmans.co.uk

Butchers with a long heritage, producing more than 70 different sausage varieties with seasonal and monthly specials.

The Dearden Tea Rooms

12 Higher Deardengate,

Haslingden,

Rossendale,

Lancashire, BB4 5QJ

Telephone: 01706 557 300

Website: www.deardentea rooms.co.uk

Tea room with a vintage ambience, serving homemade meals from breakfasts to afternoon teas, plus a huge selection of loose-leaf tea and cocktail menu.

duk-pond

9-10 Cross Street,

Preston,

Lancashire, PR1 3LT

Telephone: 01772 824988

Website: www.dukpond.co.uk

Peruvian-influenced menu that's strong on local produce, gluten-free and allergy-free alternatives.

duk-pond Chorley deli and cantina

8 Cleveland Street,

Chorley,

Lancashire, PR7 1BH

Telephone: 01257 261259

Website: www.dukpond.co.uk

Deli and tapas sharing duk-pond restaurant's homemade and locally-sourced ethos.

Exchange Coffee
24 Wellgate,
Clitheroe,
Lancashire, BB7 2DP
Telephone: 01200 442270
Website: www.exchangecoffee.co.uk

Exchange Coffee Company
13-15 Fleming Square
Blackburn
Lancashire
BB2 2DG
01254 54258
info@exchangecoffee.co.uk
Coffee roaster and tea merchant, with huge selection of freshly-roasted coffees and black, white, green and fruit teas to choose from.

Gazegill Organics
Lower Gazegill Farm,
Dancer Lane,
Rimington,
Clitheroe,
Lancashire, BB7 4EE
Telephone: 01200 445519
Website: www.gazegillorganics.co.uk
Family-run organic farm, farm shop and education project selling a comprehensive range of organic products, including raw milk, meat and vegetables produced at the farm itself.

Gibbon Bridge Hotel
Chipping near Preston,
Forest of Bowland,
Lancashire, PR3 2TQ
Telephone: 01995 61456
Website: www.gibbon-bridge.co.uk
Relaxed quality dining with a focus on home-produced and locally-sourced ingredients.

Henry's Bar and Grill
5 Henry Street,
Lytham,
Lancashire, FY8 5LE
Telephone: 01253 737111
Website: www.henrysbarandgrill.co.uk
A la carte dining packed with local ingredients and an ambience and décor with a New York steakhouse feel.

Huntley's Country Stores
Whalley Road,
Samlesbury,
Lancashire, PR5 0UN
Telephone: 01772 877123 (restaurant)
01772 877811 (food hall)
Website: www.huntleys.co.uk
Destination farm shopping village with restaurant, food hall and ice cream parlour selling quality Lancashire produce.

The Inn at Whitewell
Clitheroe,
Forest of Bowland,
Lancashire, BB7 3AT
Telephone: 01200 448222
Website: www.innatwhitewell.com
A menu majoring on local food that's enjoyed in a relaxing atmosphere where dogs are welcome too.

Made in Lancashire
Myerscough College,
Bilsborrow,
Preston,
Lancashire, PR3 0RY
Website: www.madeinlancs.co.uk
Telephone: 01995 642255
Local produce membership network, supporting producers, hospitality and retailers of Lancashire food and drink.

Mrs Dowson's Ice Cream
Hawkshaw Fold,
Longsight Road,
Clayton-le-Dale,
Blackburn,
Lancashire, BB2 7JA
Website: www.mrsdowsons.co.uk
Telephone: 01254 812407
Family-owned and run ice cream maker using milk from the family's farm and producing a rainbow of ice cream flavours with local and natural ingredients.

Nutters Restaurant
Edenfield Rd,
Norden,
Rochdale,
Lancashire, OL12 7TT
Telephone: 01706 650167
Website: www.nuttersrestaurant.co.uk
Restaurant run by celebrity chef Andrew Nutter, serving modern British food with a French influence.

Preston Business Improvement District
c/o North and Western Lancashire Chamber of Commerce
9-10 Eastway Business Village
Olivers Place,
Fulwood,
Preston,
Lancashire, PR2 9WT
Telephone: 01772 653 000 option 5
Website: www.bidpreston.co.uk
Preston city centre Business Improvement District represents businesses based in Preston city centre, supporting them via campaigns and initiatives to improve the city centre as a place to invest, work, visit and live. Key events include a thrice-annual speciality Lancashire Market and month-long Love Food, Love Preston campaign, promoting Preston's culinary offer by devising specially created menus and an annual Dine with the Stars event.

Procter's Cheeses Limited
The Cheese Warehouse,
Saunders Raike,
Chipping,
Lancashire, PR3 2QY
Telephone: 01995 61626
Website: www.kickasscheese.co.uk
Cheese factors and makers of Kick Ass Cheddar and spectacular multi-layered cheese celebration cakes.

Puddleducks Tea room
Dunsop Bridge,
Clitheroe,
Lancashire, BB7 3BB
Telephone: 01200 448241
Website: www.puddleduckscafe.co.uk
A tea room, post office and general store, bang in the centre of the UK, with a menu of traditional Lancashire favourites and Puddleducks' famous pea and ham soup.

The Red Pump Inn
Clitheroe Road
Bashall Eaves,
Clitheroe,
Lancashire, BB7 3DA
Telephone: 01254 826 227
Website: www.theredpumpinn.co.uk
Historic coaching inn specialising in steak and good home-cooked meals, with luxury bed and breakfast and yurts on site.

Samlesbury Hall
Samlesbury Hall
Preston New Road,
Samlesbury,
Preston,
Lancashire, PR5 0UP
Telephone: 01254 812010
Website: www.samlesburyhall.co.uk
Restaurant set within a stunning stately home, serving dishes packed with ingredients from its own gardens, from herbs and vegetables to honey and eggs.

The Village Tea Room at Wheelton
202 Blackburn Road,
Wheelton,
Chorley,
Lancashire, PR6 8EY
Telephone: 01254 830160
Website: www.thevillagetearoomatwheelton.co.uk
Freshly-prepared, homemade meals from breakfasts and lunches, to cakes and sweet treats, plus fabulous afternoon teas served at your table in a small wicker picnic hamper.

Visit Lancashire
Farington House,
Lancashire Enterprise Business Park,
Centurion Way,
Leyland,
Lancashire, PR26 6TW
Telephone: 01772 426450
Website: www.visitlancashire.com
Destination marketing organisation for Lancashire, promoting the county's attractions, events and food and drink.

The White Horse Edgworth
2-4 Bury Road,
Edgworth,
Bolton,
Lancashire, BL7 0AY
Telephone: 01204 852 929
Website: www.whitehorseedgworth.co.uk
Pub and restaurant, specialising in home-cooked food and real cask ale on tap.

Winedown
The Cellar,
16-18 Lancaster Road,
Preston,
Lancashire, PR1 1DA
Telephone: 01772 825290
Website: www.winedown.co.uk
Funky urban wine and cheese cellar, serving a selection of Lancashire cheeses.

The Yewtree Inn
Dill Hall Brow,
Heath Charnock,
Chorley,
Lancashire PR6 9HA
Telephone: 01257 480344
Website: www.yewtreeinnanglezarke.co.uk
A relaxed restaurant with outdoor terrace and bar, serving modern British local cuisine, with a fantastic selection of gins and locally brewed beers. The terrace provides spectacular views over Rivington and Anglezarke.

me:ze PUBLISHING

Other titles in the 'Get Stuck In' series

The Sheffield Cook Book features Baldwin's Omega, Nonna's, Ashoka, Cubana, Peppercorn and lots more.
978-0-9928981-0-6

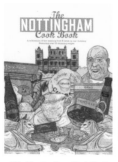

The Nottingham Cook Book features Sat Bains with Rooms, World Service, Harts, Escabeche and lots more.
978-0-9928981-5-1

The Derbyshire Cook Book features Chatsworth Estate, Fischer's of Baslow, Thornbridge Brewery and lots more.
978-0-9928981-7-5

The Cambridgeshire Cook Book features Daniel Clifford of Midsummer House, The Pint Shop, Gog Magog Hills, Clare College and lots more.
978-0-9928981-9-9

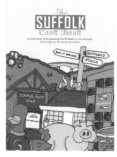

The Suffolk Cook Book features Jimmy Doherty of Jimmy's Farm, Gressingham Duck and lots more.
978-1-910863-02-2

The Manchester Cook Book features Aiden Byrne, Simon Rogan, Harvey Nichols and lots more.
978-1-910863-01-5

The Lincolnshire Cook Book features Colin McGurran of Winteringham Fields, TV chef Rachel Green, San Pietro and lots more.
978-1-910863-05-3

The Newcastle Cook Book features David Coulson of Peace & Loaf, Bealim House, Grainger Market, Quilliam Brothers and lots more.
978-1-910863-04-6

The Cheshire Cook Book features Simon Radley of The Chester Grosvenor, The Chef's Table, Great North Pie Co., Harthill Cookery School and lots more.
978-1-910863-07-7

The Leicestershire & Rutland Cook Book features Tim Hart of Hambleton Hall, John's House, Farndon Fields, Leicester Market, Walter Smith and lots more.
978-0-9928981-8-2

All books in this series are available from Waterstones, Amazon and independent bookshops.

FIND OUT MORE ABOUT US AT WWW.MEZEPUBLISHING.CO.UK